Buy Low,
Rent Smart,
Sell High

REAL ESTATE INVESTING
FOR THE LONG RUN

Scott Frank

Andy Heller

Dearborn™
Trade Publishing
A **Kaplan Professional** Company

Vice President and Publisher: Cynthia A. Zigmund
Acquisitions Editor: Mary B. Good
Senior Project Editor: Trey Thoelcke
Interior Design: Lucy Jenkins
Cover Design: Design Solutions
Typesetting: the dotted i

© 2003 by Scott Frank and Andy Heller

Published by Dearborn Trade Publishing, a Kaplan Professional Company

Printed in the United States of America

04   05   10 9 8 7 6 5 4 3 2

Library of Congress Cataloging-in-Publication Data

Frank, Scott M.
   Buy low, rent smart, sell high : real estate investing for the long run / Scott Frank, Andy Heller.
     p.   cm.
   Includes index.
   ISBN 0-7931-7756-1
   1. Residential real estate—United States.   I. Heller, Andy H.   II Title.
HD259.F7 2003
332.63′243—dc21

                                            2003010799

Dearborn Trade books are available at special quantity discounts to use for sales promotions, employee premiums, or educational purposes. Please contact our special sales department, to order or for more information, at trade@dearborn.com or 800-245-BOOK (2665), or write to Dearborn Financial Publishing, 30 South Wacker Drive, Suite 2500, Chicago, IL 60606-7481.

Scott's Dedication

This book is dedicated to the memory of my father, Denny Frank, who laid a strong foundation for me as a real estate investor and, even more important, was a great role model and father. He instilled confidence in me and taught me that you can be fair, honest, caring, respectful, and very successful in business—and anything else you set your mind to—all at the same time.

This book is also dedicated to my wonderful, loving wife, Marie, who is always there to support and encourage me, and to my four precious gifts from God, my children—Dennis, Danielle, David, and Diana—who make every day better than the previous one.

Andy's Dedication

This book is dedicated to the memory of my father, Dr. E. Maurice Heller. My father dedicated his life to helping others, becoming a leader and innovator in the field of cardiology and creator of Canada's first exercise program for recovering heart attack patients. My father was a medical man with no formal business training, yet he instilled in me a sense of fair dealing and a commitment to charity as key components of how one should live life. Additionally, my father could see the positive in almost any situation and certainly any person he encountered. Lastly, it amazed me how he was always there with the right words for any situation, whether business or personal. These are all wonderful and special qualities to spend a lifetime observing, and without his influence, I would not be where I am today.

Contents

We owe special thanks to Barbara McNichol, the Word Tripper, who always kept a positive, fun attitude while helping two rookie writers put their thoughts on paper.

We also deeply appreciate the Dearborn publishing team that helped us turn our concept for a book into a reality. We are especially grateful to Mary B. Good, Acquisitions Editor, for her willingness to publish the work of first-time authors and help us turn our concept into an outline, then a draft, and ultimately a book we're proud of.

Although the list would be too long if we mentioned everyone, we also want to thank all the great people we've had a chance to work with and get to know over the years. Here are the names of some of the people who have made our real estate business profitable, fun, and satisfying: Bernard Newson, Charles and Lisa Chandler, Bonnie Gergans, Andy Shuping, Mike Warner, Al Stewart, Sheree Berk, Eddie Scott, Fred Brown, Jacob and Cindi Gang, Jim King, Tim Sherrer, Becky Matherne, Wendy Miller, Jerome Rhodes, Mike Barry, Bob Hodge, Ruthann Davies, Debbie Johnson, and Randy Nice.

Finally, we wish to thank all of the "good" lease/purchasers we've been fortunate to learn from and to have in our lives. Again, the list is too long, but you know who you are.

From Scott. I also wish to acknowledge Ellen Frank (my mother) who has done and continues to do so much for our family, as well as Brian Frank (my brother) and Marcy Frank Cooper (my sister) who have been my real estate partners for many years and, even more important, lifelong friends. I'd also like to acknowledge Lucille and Melvin Falkof (my maternal grandparents), Ella Schechtman and Oscar Frank (my paternal grandparents), Whitney Frank (my sister-in-law), Mike Cooper (my brother-in-law), and Barry Feinberg (my stepfather), who have shared in many of my life experiences, including some in real estate. Thanks to all of you for always being there for me.

From Andy. I also wish to acknowledge my mother, Barbara Heller, who helped foster my interest in real estate and my sister for motivating me with her own entrepreneurial career as founder of Atlanta-based Circus Arts summer camp for kids. Lastly, I wish to thank a handful of life-long friends and extended family who have always been there to support and listen to me in both good and bad times. Thank you Loren, Mark, Rob, Frauline, Matt, Alon, Jens, the Nemoys, and the Starkmans.

WE'VE MADE GOOD MONEY AND SO CAN YOU

In this book, we unveil a profitable, long-term approach to real estate investing that we have developed and refined over 20 years. Our program combines the best of strict purchasing and selling (also known as flipping), strict renting (also known as landlording), and strict renting-to-own (also known as lease/purchasing). In *Buy Low, Rent Smart, and Sell High,* we'll show you how to do all of this and more.

This is *not* a "get-rich-quick" program or one that advocates creating wealth at another's expense. In fact, in the wake of dot-com flameouts, corporate scandals, and September 11, this book is for anyone who wants to invest responsibly in single-family homes in middle-American neighborhoods and generate significant, sustainable wealth over the long run. Our straightforward, time-manageable method shows you how to take control of your financial future so you can ensure your family and friends have what they need and, at the same time, have plenty of what is most valuable to them—time with *you.*

Our method makes good money for investors while making a difference for credit or cash poor Americans who cannot qualify to buy their own homes. It's the American Dream delivered responsibly for you and for them.

WHY TELL OUR SECRETS

Why are we revealing our wealth-building ideas instead of hoarding them for ourselves? Because we believe what goes around comes around. Over the years, a lot of people have shared their knowledge with us. We've been able to build on their ideas to create significant wealth responsibly and make a positive impact on many people's lives. From our experience, there are plenty of residential homes for our readers to invest in without affecting our business. It's our turn to share what we've learned so you can benefit from our experience. Our hope is that you, too, can make a difference in other people's lives while building your own real estate riches.

BUY LOW

Buying low is not about finding unsuspecting, unsophisticated, distressed sellers who are willing to sell their homes dirt cheap. Unlike some other investor programs, ours is not about finding properties that are "a steal." Fortunately, our experience reveals plenty of homes available for purchase at reasonable discounts from knowledgeable, nondistressed sellers.

To us, buy low is all about buying single-family homes at a consistent 10 to 20 percent discount from informed sellers—people who know what they're doing, primarily lenders (banks and mortgage companies). Lenders are in the business of lending money, not selling homes. Therefore, when they're forced to foreclose (which has become a much bigger problem in the new millennium, as discussed later), they allow you to buy low at a fair discount. Every time you buy a property from a lender, your real estate portfolio value will increase by the discount you receive when you acquire the property.

You'll learn more about buying low in Chapter 5, "Money for Purchasing Your Homes"; Chapter 6, "Finding Good Homes"; Chapter 7, "Making Offers and Negotiating Purchases"; and Chapter 8, "The Real Estate Purchase Contract."

RENT SMART

Renting smart is not simply about getting a tenant into your home fast so you can begin collecting rent quickly. It is about finding "good" people to rent-to-own your property in an efficient way. By applying our lease/purchase program, you should be able to attract good renters fast and get fair market rent for your property. You should also be able to minimize your time, money, and headaches.

A key point in our lease/purchase program is predicting that your renters will take much better care of the home than typical tenants do— after all, they expect to own it. Also, because the lease/purchasers have an exclusive right to home ownership, you transfer maintenance and repair responsibility to them.

We cover renting smart in Chapter 9, "Fixing Up Your Homes"; Chapter 10, "Our Lease/Purchase Program"; Chapter 11, "Marketing Your Homes"; Chapter 12, "Finding the Right Lease/Purchasers"; Chapter 13, "The Lease/Purchase Contract"; and Chapter 14, "Managing Lease/Purchase Relationships."

SELL HIGH

Just as buying low isn't about finding unsuspecting, unsophisticated buyers you can take advantage of, neither is selling high. Rather, it's about selling the home at or close to fair market value.

Unlike many homesellers who are forced to sell their homes at a discount or risk sitting on the home for many months (or even years), you can stay firm on your sales price because the lease/purchase program allows you to get a contract on the home quickly at a fair market price. Under the lease/purchase contract, you can also complete your sales transaction without paying the 5 to 7 percent commission required in most real estate sales transactions.

Most of the people attracted to lease/purchases have financial challenges, usually credit problems and/or little savings. However, it doesn't mean they won't be good tenants or they'd never be able to own a home. In many cases, they simply need time to save enough money or clean up their credit to qualify for a homeowner loan. Unlike with many other lease/purchase programs, we usually give our lease/purchaser three years or more to buy the home. Why? Because this is the time frame most people actually need to repair their credit or save a down payment. In return, these lease/purchasers are more than willing to pay the fair market value on the home.

Knowing you can sell the home at fair market value using a lease/purchase gives you additional leverage to sell it at or close to fair market value when negotiating with a straight buyer who doesn't want to rent the home first. But in either case, you're able to sell high (that is, at or close to fair market value).

As you read this book, you'll see that cash windfalls from selling homes build your real estate wealth. For every one home you sell, you'll likely have enough cash to buy two or three additional homes.

The key elements of selling high are set out in Chapter 10, "Our Lease/Purchase Program"; Chapter 11, "Marketing Your Homes"; Chapter 12, "Finding the Right Lease/Purchasers"; Chapter 13, "The Lease/Purchase Contract"; Chapter 14, "Managing Lease/Purchase Relationships"; and Chapter 15, "Selling Your Homes."

SIX PROFIT SOURCES

What makes this program special? Each property we purchase has six sources of profit, while many other programs and investors tend to rely on one, two, or three sources.

Using six profit sources in our diversified approach provides more consistency and stability over the long run, including during down economic times. These multiple profit sources also allow us to cast a wider net of potential investment properties to purchase, because we don't depend solely on finding properties at a discount of 25 percent or more.

Our six profit sources are:

1. *Profit Source One* (P1). We buy homes at a discount, typically 10 to 20 percent below fair market value. By acquiring them below market, we immediately lock in a profit upon purchase. This profit will be realized once the property is sold.
2. *Profit Source Two* (P2). We generate a positive monthly cash flow on each property, because our lease/purchase allows us to get

fair market rents that exceed our monthly mortgage payments. Our monthly rents are usually 25 to 50 percent greater than the monthly mortgage payments.

3. *Profit Source Three* (P3). We get write-offs on our tax return for interest, taxes, insurance, repairs, and other expenses commonly paid by the owner of a house, because we acquire legal ownership of our investment properties. These tax write-offs can save a lot each year.

4. *Profit Source Four* (P4). We pay down the loan on the property each month by making the monthly mortgage payment, which creates additional profit when the property is sold. While less significant than some of our other profit sources in the first few years of owning a house, the practice of paying down the loan leads to making a more substantial profit each year. If we own the house for many years, this profit can be even greater.

5. *Profit Source Five* (P5). We get appreciation value on the property whenever we own it for an extended period of time. Typically, our lease/purchasers agree to buy the homes for the fair market value they have at the time lease/purchase agreements are signed. However, if they choose not to exercise their option or need an extension, we take the opportunity to raise the sales price to the new fair market value, which includes appreciation. In a stable economy, we have seen homes in middle-income neighborhoods appreciate 2 to 5 percent a year.

6. *Profit Source Six* (P6). We get lease/purchase option money, which entitles the renter to purchase the property at a predetermined price (today's fair market value) for a preset period of time, generally three years. The option money payment is made when lease/purchase contracts are first signed. Typically, the payment is 1 percent of the property's value (e.g., $1,000 on a $100,000 home). Although we usually apply the option money toward the down payment when the lease/purchasers buy the home, we keep the money if they do not carry out the purchase.

STICKING WITH WHAT WORKS

From the viewpoint of two people who have dealt with approximately 100 homes worth more than $10 million, we've shown that consistently sticking with what works makes money. We treat each home purchase as a separate business and have never sold one at a loss. Families we've worked with have often been able to obtain home loans after just a few years on our lease/purchase program.

We've also learned that when we deviate from our own model, we pay a price . . . in profits, in convenience, in time with our families and friends, and in other important ways. At the same time, we constantly adjust our model to changing laws and market conditions. We suggest using and adapting our ideas and experience toward investing in your own backyard.

DEEP SENSE OF RESPONSIBILITY

You've probably known investors who operate with a short-term mentality and leave carcasses behind them. That approach goes against our deep sense of responsibility to the society we live in.

You may have also read other real estate investing books that detail how to "get rich quick." Rarely do these methods work as described; often, investors emulating them, and the people they work with, end up in a worse place. Using our long-term approach to investing, you can make everyone involved a winner.

We believe in treating everyone in our circle well. For us, it's not about knocking down targets in our path; it's about building long-term relationships. People know that we do business fairly, so they want to do business with us. You'll read examples throughout this book of how this philosophy has worked well for us.

HOW THIS CAN WORK FOR YOU

When you follow the steps in this book, you'll be on your way to achieving long-term, sustainable wealth. Indeed, you may find the most valuable section is the Appendix, complete with sample contracts, sample forms, and sample marketing materials. Every piece has evolved over the past two decades. These alone are well worth the investment you've made in *Buy Low, Rent Smart, and Sell High.*

As you read the chapters that follow, you'll understand the nuts and bolts of how this approach has worked for us—and how it can work for you. We've invested thousands of hours and dollars studying real estate, learning from the school of hard knocks, and perfecting our long-term model. By detailing our lessons learned, we hope you can use our tried-and-true method of making money while making a positive difference in others' lives.

If we can do it, you can too. Learn it, and you will be making the American Dream come true for yourself and many others.

1

MAKING YOUR
FIRST MILLION DOLLARS

This chapter gives a big picture explanation of our program to buy low, rent smart, and sell high. It ties together elements of other solid, wealth-building real estate programs while illustrating unique aspects of this program. At the same time, it further explains the six profit centers that help you build wealth in the long run, even through tough economic times. Once you understand this picture, you'll be better able to implement the specific steps set out in the chapters that follow.

OTHER REAL ESTATE INVESTMENT PROGRAMS

You've likely studied dozens of other real estate investment programs and books, many of which are very good. However, most of these focus on one of the two models of real estate investing shown in Figure 1.1.

Although they're built on good ideas, these models are one-dimensional in that they rely on a limited number of profit sources. For the buy low and sell programs, the profits come from the difference between the investor discount at the time of purchase and the sale of the home (our profit source one). These programs depend on finding many prop-

FIGURE 1.1   *Common Real Estate Investing Models*

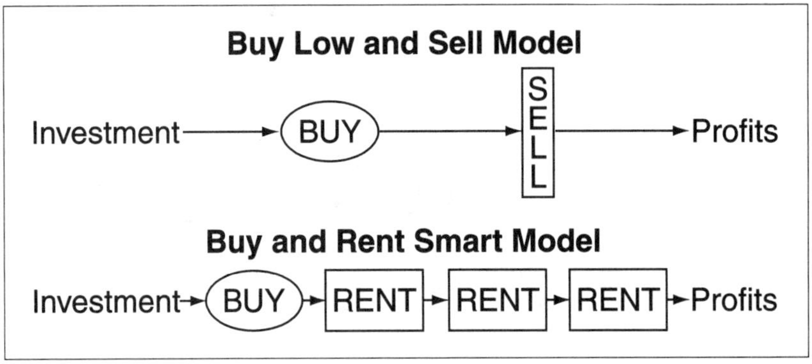

erties at steep discounts (25 percent below or more market value) or with little/no money down—assumptions we find both impractical and unrealistic for most investors with limited financial resources and/or experience.

For the buy and rent smart programs, the profits come from the steady cash flow of rents and tax write-offs (our profit sources two and three) plus the eventual rewards from paying down the loan and home appreciation (our profit sources four and five).

These programs have more stability than buy low and sell models for two reasons: they don't depend on one-time cash windfalls from sales, and there are many more homes that are slightly discounted than homes that are steeply discounted and/or available for no money down. However, these models often take much longer to grow profits because they don't have the periodic cash windfalls from selling and they come with the additional costs of time, money, and headaches when dealing with tenants.

OUR REAL ESTATE INVESTING PROGRAM

Our real estate investing program combines the profit sources of the others while adding a new one: the lease/option payment. This program allows you to grow your profits more steadily than buy low and sell programs and faster than buy and rent smart programs. It also ties together many of the buy low and rent smart elements of other programs, and it adds the sell high aspect, too.

The diagrams in Figure 1.2 illustrate how two variations of our program consistently build profits.

These models illustrate that if you follow the program, its buy low, rent smart, and sell high approach will give you a lot of control over your profits. You will have *less* control over when and if lease/purchasers buy your homes. Yet you can still win regardless of when and if your lease/purchasers exercise their options.

Example 1 illustrates how the first four profit sources (investor discount, rent, tax write-offs, and loan pay down) increase your wealth when the lease/purchaser rents for a while and then buys the home. Example 2 shows how the other two profit sources (home appreciation and option money) are unlocked when a lease/purchaser doesn't buy and you lease/purchase the home again.

FIGURE 1.2 *Our Real Estate Investing Model*

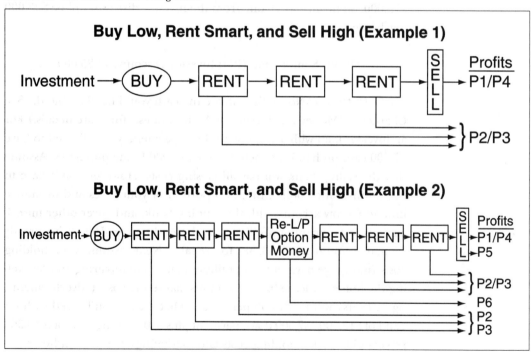

ILLUSTRATIVE EXAMPLES

Using the principles of our model, let's go through a few hypothetical examples in which we find homes to buy low, rent smart, and sell high.

Hypothetical Assumptions

Home price. For this example, assume you're consistently able to purchase $100,000 homes from a bank at a 15 percent discount. Your price is $85,000, giving you an immediate $15,000 in investor profit when you sell the home. Also, assume that each house needs repairs costing $3,500 and that the bank is willing to discount the home an additional $10,000 to cover those costs plus the time and effort you spend repairing each property. In effect, the bank sells you these homes that will have a fair market value of $100,000 (once properly repaired) for $75,000. So profit source one from the investor discount will be $25,000 per home.

Profit Source One (P1): Investor Discount = $25,000

Cash to buy. Now let's evaluate the cash you'll need on hand. (See Chapter 5, "Money for Purchasing Your Homes," for more details.) For an investor loan with a 10 percent down payment, you will need to have $7,500 cash on hand for each of your $75,000 home purchases. Assume that the selling bank will pay all closing costs. However, you'll have to buy an insurance policy, prepay a portion of your taxes and insurance into an escrow account with the lending bank, and cover other miscellaneous costs at closing. We'll say that these add up to $500. We've already estimated you'll need $3,500 for repairs. Next, assume your holding costs (mortgage payments and utilities paid while repairing and marketing the home for lease/purchase) plus marketing costs (advertisements, signs, flyers) will be $1,000 per home. That means you'll need cash on hand of $12,500 ($7,500 down payment plus $500 closing costs plus $3,500 repairs plus $1,000 holding costs and marketing) to buy each home.

Cash to Buy Each Home = $12,500
Down Payment Equity = $7,500

Cash from rent. Assume a monthly rent of $1,000 (1 percent of the value of the home) and monthly mortgage payment (PITI) of $500 ($67,500 loan at 6 to 7 percent interest over 30 years, plus taxes and insurance, paid to your bank monthly). Therefore, profit source two will have a $500 monthly positive cash flow for a total of $6,000 each year ($500/month times 12 months/year).

Profit Source Two (P2): Rent Cash Flow = $6,000/year

Tax write-off. For profit source three, annual tax write-offs, assume you're able to write off expenses related to interest, taxes, insurance, and repairs on each home. We'll ignore depreciation for this example, because you pay these back when you sell the property. Also, note that interest, taxes, and insurance expenses will have no additional impact on your cash flow because they're paid in the monthly mortgage payment and your repair expenses of $3,500 are paid prior to purchasing the home. Accordingly, assume your annual tax write-offs will be $6,000 and, therefore, you won't have to pay any taxes on the first $6,000 in rent you collect for each home during the year.

Profit Source Three (P3): Tax Write-offs = income from rent is tax-free

Loan pay down and home appreciation. For profit source four, assume you pay down the loan principal by $1,000 each year (again, a $75,000 loan at 6 to 7 percent for 30 years). For profit source five, assume each home appreciates at 2 percent per year, approximately $2,000 a year. Please note that you do not get the benefit of this particular profit source unless you lease/purchase the home again. However, a home worth $100,000 initially will have a sales price of $106,000 three years later, one of the benefits of holding real estate in a stable economy.

Profit Source Four (P4): Pay Down Loan = $1,000/year
Profit Source Five (P5): Home Appreciation = $6,000 every 3 years
   (when the home is re-lease/purchased)

Subsequent lease/purchasing costs and option money. Assume that you need to lease/purchase approximately 25 to 33 percent of your homes each year. Each time you lease/purchase, you experience a downside and an upside. The downside is the extra time and money (repairs, lost rent, holding, and marketing costs) estimated at $4,000 per home each time you lease/purchase. The upside is that you get to unlock profit source six and keep the option money, in this case $1,000 (1 percent of the value of the home). Even more important, as we just discussed, we assume the home has appreciated by 2 percent each year. So the fair market value of each of your homes appreciates by $2,000 every year, and you raise the sales price by this amount every time you re-lease/purchase the home.

Profit Source Six (P6): Option Money Kept = $1,000 (when re-L/P)
Lease/Purchase Costs = $4,000

Sales proceeds. Assume that approximately 33 to 50 percent of your homes sell to lease/purchasers in three years. Also, assume each home sells for the fair market value of $100,000 (the value of the home at the time you purchased it). One of the key components of our lease/purchase model is locking in the sales price for three years. This allows you to attract good lease/purchasers, transfer the maintenance and repair responsibilities to them, and have them pay all closing costs upon sale. You would apply the $100,000 proceeds to paying off your $67,500 loan, which has been paid down to $64,500 during the three years ($1,000/year).

Let's further assume you allow $100 of the rent each month to be applied to the down payment. So after three years, you give your lease/purchasers $3,600 when they exercise their purchase option and buy your home. Having this applied rent element provides incentive for the lease/purchaser to take care of the home, pay rent on time, and exercise the option to buy.

Unfortunately, as you build your wealth, Uncle Sam gets a piece of it, estimated at $7,000, based on a 28 percent tax bracket times the $25,000 investor discount, your capital gains on the sale. (For this example, we've ignored 1031 Exchanges, which could defer some of the tax obligations—see your accountant for more information on 1031 Exchanges.) Ultimately, for every sale of a home, you'll come away with cash of approximately $25,000 (made up of $100,000 sales price minus $64,500 loan balance minus $3,600 total of applied rent minus $7,000 capital gains taxes) to use for purchasing more investment homes.

Cash from Each Sale: $25,000

Additional items. For simplicity, let's assume all purchases, sales, and re-lease/purchases occur on January 1 of each year. Also, let's ignore the likely benefits of rent increases, interest collected on bank accounts, increases in taxes and insurance, and other positive and negative nominal dollars (which will essentially offset each other or be positive over time).

FIGURE 1.3 *Profits from a Single Home*

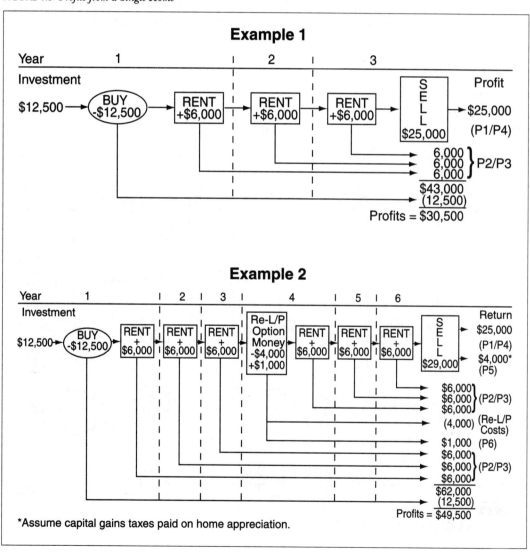

Profits from a Single Home

The examples in Figure 1.3 illustrate the profits you can recognize from buying, renting, and selling a single home.

As both examples indicate, our program positions you to make significant profits. In Example 1, a $12,500 investment was turned into more than $40,000 in three years, making almost $30,000 in profits. In Example 2, the same investment turned into more than $60,000 in six years and approximately $50,000 in profits. This isn't too shabby for a single home in which you buy low, rent smart, and sell high.

FIGURE 1.4 *First Five Years*

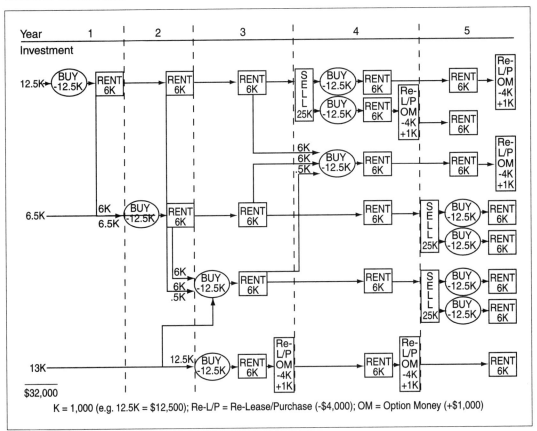

FIGURE 1.5 *Ten Years: Houses Bought, Sold, Rented*

Year	1	2	3	4	5	6	7	8	9	10
Total Homes to Start Year	0	1	2	4	6	8	10	12	14	16
Buy	1	1	2	3	4	5	6	7	8	9
Sell	(0)	(0)	(0)	(1)	(2)	(3)	(4)	(5)	(6)	(7)
Total Homes at Year End	1	2	4	6	8	10	12	14	16	18
Homes Re-Lease/Purchased	0	0	1	2	2	2	2	3	3	4
Homes Bought (cumulative)	1	2	4	7	11	16	22	29	37	46
Homes Sold (cumulative)	0	0	0	1	3	6	10	15	21	28
Homes Re-L/P (cumulative)	0	0	1	3	5	7	9	12	15	18

Profits from Multiple Homes

How can an initial cash investment of approximately $30,000 (over three years) grow into more than $1,000,000 in less than ten years? By adding more homes to the investment model. For this example, we'll assume you start out buying one home each year for the first two years, buy two homes in year three, buy three homes in year four, and increase your purchases by buying one more than the preceding year.

Please note: The example in Figure 1.5 is intended to illustrate the potential of our real estate investment program if applied properly and consistently over time. In no way is it meant to predict or guarantee future success, which is influenced by such factors as the homes you're able to buy, economic fluctuations, changes in home values in particular communities, and even individual aptitude for putting this program in place.

OUR PHILOSOPHY

Yes, there are many ways to generate significant wealth from real estate. However, our program provides a consistent and stable means for the average person to do so. Our philosophy is simply to buy homes at a discount (usually from banks) and use our lease/purchase program to rent them easily and sell at fair market value. Tying these simple steps together with our suggestions on how to evaluate and market homes, do repairs, use contracts, and so on helps you unlock the six profit sources to build wealth with real estate.

We suggest that you start slowly to get comfortable with our program and that you be consistent in your use of our model. When you buy low, rent smart, and sell high, you'll build significant wealth for the long run. We wish you the best of luck in making your first million dollars.

FIGURE 1.6 *Ten-Year Example: Cash Flow*

Year	1	2	3	4	5	6	7	8	9	10
"Cash" Infusion	12,500	6,500	13,000	0	0	0	0	0	0	0
"Cash" to Buy (Buy)	(12,500)	(12,500)	(25,000)	(37,500)	(50,000)	(62,500)	(75,000)	(87,500)	(100,000)	(112,500)
Down Payment Equity (DPE)	7,500	15,000	30,000	45,000	60,000	75,000	90,000	105,000	120,000	135,000
Profits from Investor Discount (P1)	25,000	50,000	100,000	150,000	200,000	250,000	300,000	350,000	400,000	450,000
Profits from Monthly Rent Cash Flow (P2)	6,000	12,000	24,000	36,000	48,000	60,000	72,000	84,000	96,000	108,000
Profits from Tax Write-offs (P3)	rent is tax-free	rent is tax-free	rent is tax-free	rent is tax-free	rent is tax-free	rent is tax-free	rent is tax-free	rent is tax-free	rent is tax-free	rent is tax-free
Profits from Paying Down Loan (P4)	1,000	3,000	7,000	10,000	13,000	16,000	19,000	22,000	25,000	28,000
Profits from Home Appreciation (P5)	0	0	0	4,000	12,000	20,000	28,000	36,000	44,000	52,000
Profits from Option Money (P6)	0	0	1,000	2,000	2,000	2,000	2,000	3,000	3,000	4,000
Costs to Re-Lease/ Purchase (RLP)	0	0	(4,000)	(8,000)	(8,000)	(8,000)	(8,000)	(12,000)	(12,000)	(16,000)
Proceeds from Sale (Sale)	0	0	0	25,000	50,000	75,000	100,000	125,000	150,000	175,000
Your "Cash" in Bank (Cash Start – Buy + Sale + P2 + P3 + P6 – RLP)	6,000	12,000	21,000	38,500	80,500	147,000	238,000	350,500	487,500	646,000
Your "Equity" in Homes (DPE +P1 + P4 +P5)	33,500	68,000	137,000	209,000	285,000	361,000	437,000	513,000	589,000	665,000
Net Worth (Cash in Bank + Equity in Homes)	$39,500	$80,000	$158,000	$247,500	$365,500	$508,000	$675,000	$863,500	$1,076,500	$1,311,000

FIGURE 1.7 *Ten Years: Cash Flow (Supporting Calculations)*

Year	1	2	3	4	5	6	7	8	9	10
"Cash" Infusion	12.5K	6.5K	13K	0	0	0	0	0	0	0
"Cash" to Buy (Buy)	1×12.5K	1×12.5K	2×12.5K	3×12.5K	4×12.5K	5×12.5K	6×12.5K	7×12.5K	8×12.5K	9×12.5K
Down Payment Equity (DPE)	1×7.5K	2×7.5K	4×7.5K	6×7.5K	8×7.5K	10×7.5K	12×7.5K	14×7.5K	16×7.5K	18×7.5K
Profits from Investor Discount (PI)	1×25K	2×25K	4×25K	6×25K	8×25K	10×25K	12×25K	14×25K	16×25K	18×25K
Profits from Monthly Rent Cash Flow (P2)	1×6K	2×6K	4×6K	6×6K	8×6K	10×6K	12×6K	14×6K	16×6K	18×6K
Profits from Tax Write-offs (P3)	6K–6K	12K–12K	24K–24K	36K–36K	48K–48K	60K–60K	72K–72K	84K–84K	96K–96K	108K–108K
Profits from Paying Down Loan (P4)	1×1K	2K+1K	3K+2K+ 1K+1K	3K+2K+ 2K+1K+ 1K+1K	3K+2K+ 2K+1K+ 1K+1K+1K	13K+3K	16K+3K	19K+3K	22K+3K	25K+3K
Profits from Home Appreciation (P5)	0	0	0	1×4K	4K+4K+4K	5×4K	7×4K	9×4K	11×4K	13×4K
Profits from Option Money (P6)	0	0	0	1×1K	2×1K	2×1K	2×1K	3×1K	3×1K	4×1K
Costs to Re-Lease/ Purchase (RLP)	0	0	0	1×4K	2×4K	2×4K	2×4K	3×4K	3×4K	4×4K
Proceeds from Sale (Sale)	0	0	1×25K	1×25K	2×25K	3×25K	4×25K	5×25K	6×25K	7×25K
Your "Cash" in Bank (Cash Start – Buy + Sale + P2 + P3 + P6 – RLP)	12.5K– 12.5K+0 +6K+0	(6K+6.5K) –12.5K+0 +12K+0 +0–0	(12K+13K) –25K+0 +24K+0 +1K–4K	21K– 37.5K+25K +36K+0 +2K–8K	38.5K– 50K+50K +48K+0 +2K–8K	80.5K– 62.5K+75K +60K+0 +2K–8K	147K– 75K+100K +72K+0 +2K–8K	238K– 87.5K+125K +84K+0 +3K–12K	350.5K– 100K+150K +96K+0 +3K–12K	487.5K– 112.5K+ 175K+108K+ 0+4K–16K
	6K+	12K+	21K+	38.5K+	80.5K+	147K+	238K+	350.5K+	487.5K+	646K+
Your "Equity" in Homes (DPE +PI + P4 +P5)	7.5K+ 25K+ 1K+0	15K+ 50K+ 3K+0	30K+ 100K+ 7K+0	45K+ 150K+ 10K+4K	60K+ 200K+ 13K+12K	75K+ 250K+ 16K+20K	90K+ 300K+ 19K+28K	105K+ 350K+ 22K+36K	120K+ 400K+ 25K+44K	135K+ 450K+ 28K+52K
	33.5K	68K	137K	209K	285K	361K	437K	513K	589K	665K
Net Worth (Cash in Bank + Equity in Homes)	6K+ 33.5K	12K+68K	21K+ 137K	38.5K+ 209K	80.5K+ 285K	147K+ 361K	238K+ 437K	350.5K+ 513K	487.5K+ 589K	646K+ 665K

2

GETTING STARTED

What does it take to be a successful real estate investor? How much knowledge, time, and money do you need? Can you do it part-time and still be successful? This chapter gives you some key insights into getting started with our real estate investment program.

THE THREE ESSENTIALS

1. Knowledge

Having sound knowledge of the real estate industry and a solid business plan are essential for succeeding as a real estate investor. You can gain knowledge primarily through research and experience, and you should do much of your research before you take your first step. To get started, read books, join a real estate investment club, and talk to other real estate investors in your community (in Atlanta, for example, the Georgia Real Estate Investors Association). Others' experiences and insights—combined with what you learn from this book—are the first big steps in developing real estate investment knowledge. Over the years, you'll naturally gain even greater knowledge from your own experiences. Remember: Don't ever stop studying, listening, and learning.

Before we became partners, Scott already had been in real estate for about ten years, so he brought a great deal of knowledge to the partnership. However, Scott had never purchased a foreclosure from a bank or sold a home using a lease/purchase. Before purchasing our first property together, we did considerable research (see Chapter 3, "Our Story, Goals, and Niche") on foreclosures and lease/purchases. We studied, listened, and learned to develop the knowledge necessary for success in this business.

2. Time

Making big money in real estate doesn't necessarily take a lot of time, but it does take consistency. This means consistently devoting time to your real estate investing business and backing it with a strong commitment. It's possible to operate most of this business on weekends and weekday evenings without compromising your full-time job. We know this because we've done it that way.

When you have to make calls to banks, lease/purchasers, repair people, and others during business hours, simply take a few minutes during your lunch or break to handle them. Have a dedicated phone number with voice mail for your real estate business, and make it the only number you give out. This way, the voice-mail takes messages so you can pick your own times to call people back. You'll find hints about using your time most efficiently throughout this book.

We recommend committing five to ten hours a week toward this venture. Your time commitment may or may not increase as your portfolio increases. If you apply our methods and select the right properties and lease/purchasers, many of your homes will become cash cows sustained on autopilot. We are both proof that a substantial portfolio can be managed while maintaining full-time day jobs. On occasion, we've used real estate agents and others to assist with certain management tasks, but not before we'd established a base portfolio and had a positive cash flow to cover these costs.

3. Money

Since the early 1990s, when we formed our partnership, lending practices have become more relaxed and investor financing options have multiplied. Still, the biggest obstacle to getting started in real estate investing tends to be financing. That said, you *can* get into this business with the money you need for the down payment on your first house, plus funds for repairs and marketing. You may also find opportunities to acquire properties with very little or no money down.

In today's investor lending market, a down payment is usually 10 percent of the purchase price. For a home valued at $100,000 in good condition but needing some repairs, this translates into $8,000 on an $80,000 purchase price (a 15 percent discount plus $5,000 off for repairs). Remember, you'll have to pay for those $5,000 in repairs and other related costs, so you may need closer to $15,000 in cash to get the home lease/purchased. (See Chapter 7, "Making Offers and Negotiating Purchases," for details on estimating the money you'll need.) Exact numbers depend on the prices of single-family homes in the neighborhoods you're targeting and the extent of repairs needed. However, as our examples show, it is possible to buy and lease/purchase your first property with less than $10,000 in hand, if homes in your target neighborhood sell for $100,000 or less. Similarly, you may need $20,000 for houses selling for $200,000, and so on. You'll see ways to maximize available cash later in this book.

You'll need to work with banks and mortgage companies to secure investor loans as you get started. Home equity loans on your primary residence may also come in handy. Later, once profits come in, it's smart to keep pouring them back into your business so you can benefit from the buying power of cash. Our motto is: Cash Is King. (See Chapter 5, "Money for Purchasing Your Homes.")

We recognize that not many people will draw against all of their equity in their home or throw all of their savings into a method they read about in a book. That's why we suggest starting slowly and investing carefully until you feel comfortable.

PART-TIME VERSUS FULL-TIME

Real estate can be an ideal way to substantially supplement your income while maintaining your full-time job. We suggest you get your feet wet one house at a time. Moving slowly has been our experience, and we contend it's essential for other new investors, too. So follow our method as you work full-time and test, test, test as you go along.

Why do we suggest going slowly in the early stages? Because you want to:

- Minimize your financial risks and avoid getting into trouble. Keeping your full-time job will act as a safety net.
- Learn how to find good homes (see Chapter 6) and set up your real estate team (see Chapter 4), get comfortable with this method, and realize some income before plunging into this full-time.
- Funnel all early proceeds back into your real estate business for ongoing investments rather than pay yourself a salary or commission.
- Allow the assets in your company to grow steadily so you can build cash reserves. Over time, you'll gain negotiating power that comes from using cash in your transactions. Remember our motto: Cash Is King.

If you eventually want to make real estate your full-time vocation (and our program does serve as the basis for that), we believe your success will depend on the three essentials of knowledge, time, and money. Of course, when you're doing this full-time you'll have the time. However, many real estate investors make mistakes in not having their *knowledge* and *money* bases covered well.

Knowledge. Have you become confident and familiar with the process we've outlined in this book? It is much easier to make the inevitable mistakes if you have a regular job to fall back on for income and day-to-day obligations. Mistakes cost money—money you may need to survive once you depend on real estate full-time. Everyone is different, but you will likely gain confidence after you have successfully acquired, fixed up, and lease/purchased five to ten homes.

Money. Do you have the cash flow from your present asset base—including, but not limited to, the properties you have already acquired—to support yourself full-time in this venture? Can you secure investor loans based on your present asset base and overall financial picture? Or do you have an available and dependable source for cash (i.e., either you presently possess it or can access it through a reliable, committed investor)?

FINDING YOUR FIRST PROPERTY

Over the years, we've tried a number of different ways to locate good deals. The way we currently find most of our homes is by working with lenders (banks and mortgage companies) who foreclose on properties. These sellers are in business to lend money, not sell properties, so they are often willing to sell at a reasonable discount to get foreclosed homes off their books. As an investor, this gives you peace of mind, because you don't have to purchase discounted properties from distressed sellers (e.g., families who are down on their luck) or unsophisticated sellers (e.g., people who should probably use a real estate agent to represent them). Lenders are smart businesspeople who are willing to sell to you at a discount for a specific business reason—to get their money out of the property so they can lend it to someone else.

We found our first properties by following foreclosure notices in the local newspaper (in Georgia, the lender must advertise for four weeks before foreclosing). Later, we developed relationships with many of the lenders as well as real estate agents who specialize in selling these types of properties. We did it and so can you. (See Chapter 6, "Finding Good Homes.")

LEASE/PURCHASING YOUR FIRST PROPERTY

We bought our first home together in Atlanta in the early 1990s. Our initial idea was to fix up this house and flip it (resell it quickly for a profit). For several months, we advertised the house for sale and got little response. But when we advertised it for lease/purchase—bingo—within two weeks, we attracted many inquiries and found a great family for our home. We realized that by renting to responsible people who intended to buy our home, we created a win-win situation: we could make good money, and good people could own our homes within a few years.

We compared the economics of flipping properties versus this lease/purchase method. To make a satisfactory profit by flipping, investors often need to purchase properties at a 20 to 25 percent discount or more. Flippers need this discount, because selling the property could take several months or longer, so they could spend a lot on utility bills, mortgage payments, advertising costs, etc., until the home sells (and then they may have to sell it at a 5 to 10 percent discount).

Using our lease/purchase model, you, the investor, can make a healthy profit with only a 10 to 20 percent discount. You set the sales price in the lease/purchase contract at the current fair market value of the property. The lease/purchaser is thrilled, because the price of the home is fair *and* it's locked in for three years. This enables you to sell the property at fair market value without having to discount it. Of particular importance, because the lease/purchase terms are extremely fair (much more fair than many you see elsewhere, as discussed in Chapter 10), you can feel good about how you treat your lease/purchaser in this win-win scenario.

Because it generally takes more time, effort, and money to sell a house than to rent it, our model emphasizes keeping the cash flowing by getting good people into the house as quickly as possible. Our average marketing time has been fine-tuned to two or three weeks; it's difficult to find a program with a lower time-to-market than ours.

As for the headaches and costs that come from renting homes until they get purchased, our lease/purchase program minimizes these. If the renters actually intend to buy the homes, they are likely to take better care of them and pay their rent on time. We usually get a nice monthly positive cash flow from the rent, because it's generally 25 to 50 percent greater than the mortgage payment. In this program, we transfer all repair responsibilities to the renters (after a reasonable warranty period of about three months). After all, when they sign the lease/purchase contract, in many ways it's like they own the home. We can't sell it to anyone else, and they get the full benefit of any improvements they make to the home. This is what we mean by creating cash cows on autopilot. (See Chapter 10, "Our Lease/Purchase Program," for more details.)

MARKETING YOUR FIRST PROPERTY

We waste no time beginning our marketing program. In fact, we often begin advertising the house's availability even before we close on it. We know from experience that the majority of calls come from ads we run on the weekends, so we want to put ads in the local newspaper two weekends in a row before our first showing. Many communities have a Sunday pullout real estate section. While calls often come in during the week, many come in from our ads listed in the previous Sunday's pullout section.

Here's an example of how we minimize time-to-market, not wasting a single day in the process. We sign a contract to buy a house on Monday, the fourth of the month. The property needs approximately one week for completing repairs and improvements, so we place an ad in the local newspaper beginning Saturday the second. First thing Monday after the closing, repairs begin on the property, and we place our FOR LEASE/PURCHASE sign in the front yard. By Saturday the ninth, repairs and improvements are 80 to 90 percent complete. We have legally owned the property for only five or six days, yet because of the advertising, we now have almost two full weekends of calls plus several from posting the sign.

We begin returning these calls on Saturday the ninth through the morning of Sunday the tenth and set up appointments to show the property on the afternoon of the 10th. Although the property is not completely finished, enough of the repairs and improvements are complete that the prospective lease/purchasers are able to see the quality of the work in progress. If someone shows concern about the uncompleted work, we explain that we're only two or three days away from finishing. Before any deal is signed, they'll have the opportunity to view the home again once all the work has been finished. We collect one to three applications on Sunday the 10th; by the 13th, we've picked out the lease/purchaser we want to move into our home. In this example, we've owned a house (needing a week for repairs) for only nine days and already have lined up a lease/purchaser. We've had many successful experiences similar to this one. (See Chapter 11, "Marketing Your Homes," for more about the strategy we use.)

FINDING GOOD LEASE/PURCHASERS

The candidates for our lease/purchase program typically don't have good credit or much money; otherwise, they'd be buying a home the conventional way. Usually, they come to us at a time when they are challenged financially. We seek out people who are honest about their financial situation and also have a decent rental history and solid employment. Sometimes we get an additional security deposit to cover our risk.

Here's our process. Once we've selected promising applicants, we take about three business days to review applications, send them off to a credit agency, get reports back from the agency, and make calls on tenancy and employment history. The company that does our credit reports can also verify employment and tenancy history, but we've found it's better to do background checks ourselves. Why? When talking with employers and former landlords, it's critical to listen to their tone of voice and ask follow-up questions. We want to make sure anyone we do a lease/purchase with has solid employment and a reasonably good track record of paying rent on time. We also talk to prospective lease/purchasers throughout the process—when they first call about the home, when they fill out the application, and at least one more time on the telephone—before selecting them.

Because most people in our target audience have had trouble with credit or may have little cash, the risk for us can be higher than for other investors. That's why we want to feel good about the people we pick before we sign any contracts and allow them to live in our properties. We want to clearly emphasize this point: as property owners, we believe it's *critical* to do our own selection and management, creating solid relationships as we go. It's like restaurants that have absentee owners; they rarely operate as well as those managed day in and day out by owners.

For one lease/purchaser—a divorced, single mom with long-term employment who had lived in an apartment for over six years—it took some arm-twisting to get information from her landlord. He initially told us she had 20 instances of late payments. Yet she had stayed there for six years plus, so we sensed that the situation couldn't be that bad or she would have been kicked out earlier on. She confirmed the late payments but stated that most were only a few days late. We called the landlord back and, with a little prodding, learned that was true.

The complex where she lived did everything by the book, and her payments weren't seriously late. She could explain what had happened on those occasions. So to offset the risk we saw of signing a contract with her, we asked for a security deposit equal to three months' rent instead of one month. If she paid on time for the next 12 months, she would receive a refund equal to one month of the security deposit. This gave her an opportunity to systematize her payment schedule and satisfied us that we would probably have a good lease/purchaser. Based on this example and others, we wouldn't be as successful as we are at getting good lease/purchasers if we didn't make the calls ourselves to find out about their circumstances.

Doing our own background research and firsthand evaluations allows us to "lift the hood and inspect the engine." Then we're better able to decide whether people are likely to work out for us. (See Chapter 12, "Finding the Right Lease/Purchasers," for details on how to select good lease/purchasers, a critical part of our success.)

OUR PHILOSOPHY

Our philosophy is to be systematic in the way we execute our real estate business model. Each step makes a difference in our ability to realize a good profit while also making the most of our time and money. In the chapters that follow, we'll continue to share our knowledge. We hope you're able to use it to build your own wealth from real estate by buying low, renting smart, and selling high.

3

OUR STORY, GOALS, AND NICHE

Learning the real estate business over the past 20 years taught us many real-life lessons, mostly good and some bad. Our goal throughout this book is to share our stories so you can follow what we've done and benefit from the knowledge, experience, and most important, the lessons to be learned from "Scott and Andy's School of Hard Knocks."

A BRIEF HISTORY OF OUR PARTNERSHIP

We met in 1990. At the time, we were both in our 20s, had full-time jobs, and were working toward our graduate degrees at night. As we formed a close friendship, we brainstormed ways to partner in real estate investing. Scott had already been investing in real estate for approximately ten years, beginning with purchasing his first residential home with his father when he was a teenager. Then his dad died in a car accident in the mid-1980s, and he took over responsibility for approximately 20 residential investment properties. Andy had never invested in real estate but had dabbled in other entrepreneurial activities, and he had always looked at real estate as a solid way to make money. Both of us loved playing Monopoly growing up—we still play it—and especially liked buying, renting, and selling properties to make big money.

Realizing we needed the three essentials—knowledge, time, and money—to get our real estate partnership going, we assessed our situation. Andy had a lot of time and a little money, but he didn't have much real estate investing knowledge. Scott had a lot of knowledge and some money, but he didn't have much time because he was still in graduate school and holding down a full-time job. We both had a serious interest in real estate, a drive to be financially independent, good credit, and a strong sense of responsibility—both about our finances and about the people we did business with.

Because of our friendship, we had already developed respect, trust, and confidence in one another. And we recognized our complementary strengths. What's more, we realized our different temperaments created an ideal mix: Andy has a tendency toward risk taking and a bias toward action, while Scott has a conservative bent and tends to be methodical and careful.

Within a year of forming our partnership in 1990, we bought our first investment home. We initially tried to flip it with a quick sale, but after several months of having the house on the market, nothing was happening.

Scott had become familiar with the lease/purchasing concept from talking with other real estate investors. He had always rented his father's properties and, no matter how carefully he screened applicants, he'd never been able to secure tenants who took care of the property as if they owned it (or intended to own it). He had also experienced his share of landlord headaches such as being awakened in the middle of the night because of a burst pipe, chasing down late rents, etc. His tenants also tended to move out every one or two years, resulting in added aggravation, time, and cost related to rerenting the properties.

After talking it over, we decided to do a lease/purchase on this first home. We concluded that we could probably get the home rented much more quickly than we could sell it and start putting some cash back into our pockets. We could get a good rent with positive cash flow now and sell the home at a fair price later. Also, unlike pure rentals, the lease/purchase terms would probably attract a different caliber of tenant who would take better care of the property and reliably pay rent. After all, they intended to own the home and had a lot more at risk. In addition, the lease/purchase program would allow us to transfer repair responsibilities (after a warranty period) to the lease/purchasers, because the home essentially became theirs; we couldn't sell the home to anyone else. Because the tenant would probably become the buyer, we also wouldn't have to worry about the headaches, time, and money associated with rerenting the home.

After deciding to take the lease/purchase plunge on our first home, we placed an ad for lease/purchase and got several responses. Within two weeks, we had selected a family and signed a lease/purchase contract. This was the first of many lease/purchase agreements we have signed as partners.

We started slowly but, encouraged by our successes, we developed a practical model of helping deserving people own their own homes through lease/purchasing. We now have dealt with approximately 100 homes in the metro Atlanta area and are living proof that the real estate investing model in this book really works.

OUR GOALS

Our motivation at first was straightforward: we wanted to supplement the incomes from our full-time jobs. Over time, though, we wanted to ensure financial stability for our families. Working for corporations didn't guarantee us a financially strong future, especially in down eco-

R e a l - L i f e E x a m p l e

THE TERMITE-INFESTED HOUSE

We had made an offer on a property that seemed like a really good deal. Our offer was accepted, so we handed over our earnest money and initiated a loan application. Wisely, we had made the offer contingent on the results of a termite inspection. (We have a trustworthy termite inspector who inspects and maintains the termite bonds on all our properties.) The inspector found the house infested with termites and told us the floors were about to fall through. Due to the contingency clause in the contract, we were easily able to pull out of this deal and avoid falling into a money pit.

On the flip side, we have also faced many predictions of gloom and doom where the situation actually wasn't as bad as it first seemed.

nomic times. Knowing our supplemental income could become *essential* income in a poor economy, we decided to set goals for ourselves and take control of our financial destiny.

We studied, we attended seminars, we talked to a lot of investors. We saw that if we could get proficient at finding deals on residential homes, picking good lease/purchasers, and building a strong support team, we could make our dreams of financial independence come true.

Like the game Monopoly, buying real estate and renting houses can position investors to attain great wealth. However, we didn't jump into this business too quickly. We knew if we made significant purchasing mistakes, we could also buy ourselves into a nightmare. On the one hand, you can invest less than $10,000 in cash and then—low and behold— own a piece of real estate that has an appraised value of $100,000. This gives you the opportunity to make a fabulous return on your initial $10,000 investment. On the other hand, it also represents tremendous potential for costly problems. If you invest $10,000 in the stock market and, in the worse case, the company goes belly-up, your maximum potential

A *n o t h e r* R *e a l - L i f e* E *x a m p l e*

THE FALLING AWAY CHIMNEY

In this case, a general home inspector told us repairs on a certain house would run $20,000 or more, because the chimney was falling away from the structure and the floors were falling in. Something didn't ring true about that report, so we got a second opinion from a foundation specialist. He told us the leaning chimney was not a big deal, that it would only cost $2,000 to fix. And, he said, every house settles to some degree. In this case, the floors were fine. From that, we learned that sometimes we need more than one opinion to help us make the right decisions.

Also, we quickly learned the value of repeatedly working with knowledgeable people to give us advice and service. Yes, we have met some we'd never work with again, but over time we've put together a reliable team. We recommend sourcing top attorneys, accountants, insurance agents, mortgage lenders, home contractors—professionals at the top of their game who understand the local market. The good ones share our philosophy: they know their business and are eager to do well through creating trusting, long-term relationships.

loss is the $10,000 you invested. However, in real estate, while you can gain more than your initial $10,000, you can also lose significantly more than your investment if you make serious mistakes. Therefore, this powerful investment vehicle must be handled carefully.

The examples of the termite-infested house and the falling away chimney support our philosophy of prudent growth. One saved us a small fortune; the other added to our fortunes.

OUR NICHE

One of the strengths of our program is *knowing our niche* inside and out. This has evolved over time based on our experience and teachings from others.

Single-Family Homes in Middle-Income Neighborhoods

We've selected single-family homes in middle-income neighborhoods (for us, the metro Atlanta area) as our preferred type of real estate investment. Although our typical lease/purchasers tend to have bad credit or little cash, these homes tend to attract good, stable people with solid jobs and rental histories. On the other hand, we have found low-income neighborhoods to be too transient and unstable, while high-income communities tend not to have a big enough pool of people seeking lease/purchases.

If we deviate at all from our niche—if we get away from our area of expertise—we waste time and money. For example, once we investigated developing a subdivision. We had selected a builder, looked into financing, and researched easements and particulars of the land we intended to develop. A trusted real estate agent pointed out a number of concerns about the land that we hadn't yet thought about. We realized we were dabbling in unfamiliar territory—deviating from our niche, so we didn't pursue this.

Another time, one of our trusted real estate agents brought an opportunity to our attention. An older home had been built in an odd configuration in a desirable, trendy neighborhood. With an investment of $60,000 to $70,000, it could be developed into a functional duplex. The potential to make money existed, but we would have dealt with a host of other issues uncommon to our lease/purchase homes (e.g., renting and rerenting frequently, zoning issues, and so on). Again, we would not have been sticking to our niche, so we backed off.

Getting Away from Our Niche

In our early investing years, a longtime friend of Andy's approached him about paying to use our real estate sources and process to find a discounted home for his family. At this point, we had walked away from a number of great home purchases. We were doing what we recommend doing—getting into this business slowly and carefully. This offer sounded like a good opportunity to increase our revenues while helping him out. On the surface, it was another win-win scenario.

Because this person was a friend, Andy did not formalize every detail. He made a verbal agreement that if we found a discounted home and assigned the contract to him, our commission would be 50 percent of a normal real estate commission (based on the acquisition price, not the market value).

Soon after, we found the right home for Andy's friend, so he bought it. However, the friend paid us substantially less than the 50 percent commission. Andy called and left a message about it. No return call. He mailed an invoice but received neither a phone call nor a payment. When Andy finally spoke to this friend, he had a case of "amnesia" and recalled that the agreed-upon commission was lower than 50 percent. Several years later, we eventually settled on an amount lower than the 50 percent.

The result was that, even though Andy's friend saved close to $30,000, a longtime relationship was negatively affected. What lessons did we learn from this? We learned three big ones.

1. Be careful and meticulous when doing business with friends. Specifically, avoid doing business with friends except under special circumstances.
2. Keep a low profile about our real estate business. (From that time forward, we chose not to publicize our growing real estate business with casual friends and asked those who knew about our investments to respect our privacy and keep the information to themselves.)

3. Do lots of research and make a careful decision when you *don't* stick to your niche.

The bottom line is, though there are plenty of ways to make money in real estate, getting away from your niche can be costly. As you achieve some success, you will find that others (agents, attorneys, even contractors) will begin to bring various opportunities to your attention. Many of these opportunities could represent true earnings potential outside of your niche. We are certainly *not* saying to shut the door on all of them. But know the value of sticking to what works, establishing a formula, and perfecting it so that investments work right for you. Any time you take on a project that differs from what you're good at, remember the three essentials. These opportunities have a learning curve (you need more *knowledge*), will require more effort (you need more *time*), and will have hidden costs (you need more *money*).

Sticking with Our Highly Focused Niche

This book describes our highly focused niche: single-family homes in middle-income neighborhoods. On the buying end, we focus our purchases on foreclosed properties from lenders (banks and mortgage companies), allowing us to purchase somewhere between retail-priced homes (listed with an agent and sold for fair market value) and wholesale-priced homes (foreclosed on by banks and purchased by investors with deep pockets). On the selling end, we focus our efforts on attracting purchasers using our lease/purchase program. This program allows us to get good people into the home and get cash flowing quickly. It also allows us to sell the home at fair market value and have minimal headaches during the purchasing period. As a result, we tend to get good people who need time to fix their credit or accumulate cash. We have identified a highly focused niche and stuck to it as our primary investment vehicle.

Up to this point, we have chosen not to deviate from our niche while continually improving our model, but we may pursue other real estate investment vehicles in the future. If we do, we will carefully scrutinize them. Regardless of whether you adopt our niche and follow the program described in this book, we highly encourage you to read other books, talk to investors, attend seminars, and gain as much knowledge as possible so you can carefully develop *your niche.*

OUR PHILOSOPHY

Our original goal was never to do real estate full time but to simply supplement our career incomes. Yet (as you will see in Chapter 5, "Money for Purchasing Your Homes"), our day jobs made financing our real estate investments possible. We also made the decision to grow slowly, only using our own money (that is, no outside investors) because with slower growth we could have 100 percent control of our investments.

Over time, our business has grown; we've been able to sell numerous properties and significantly increase our wealth. We now have enough money and properties and, most important, the program to make this business full time, that's quite an evolution for two guys who originally only wanted to supplement their day jobs.

Clearly, we've achieved our goal (and then some) to supplement our incomes. But this real estate investment business has also evolved into much more: developing relationships and earning the respect of people in our real estate circle. Our unique program has enabled us to enjoy all of these benefits.

4

SETTING UP YOUR REAL ESTATE TEAM

Who needs to be on your real estate team? Where do you find them? What should you look for in good team members? How do you keep these people on your team? This chapter helps you build a successful team.

Putting together a dependable real estate team that supports your interests is a high priority. From all members of your team, you want honesty, flexibility, and dependability. And, of course, you want them all to be easy to do business with and cost-effective.

This chapter describes some of the essential people you will need to have on your team.

ATTORNEY

- Seek a good attorney with a background or subspecialty in real estate.
- Ask for referrals from real estate investors you respect and/or other trustworthy lawyers. Make sure the one you choose specializes in real estate law and is familiar with local laws.

- Lawyers you work with need to be competent and knowledgeable in real estate, be willing to provide guidance and share their contacts in the community.

ACCOUNTANT

- Seek a reputable accountant familiar with real estate investments, specifically single-family homes on a lease/purchase basis.
- Find an accountant who is competent and knowledgeable in real estate and willing to provide guidance.
- Other real estate investors and real estate attorneys are the best sources of referrals for accountants.
- If you plan eventually to purchase at least two properties each year, you should make sure your accountant is familiar with section 1031 of the tax code, also referred to as 1031 Exchanges, which essentially allows you to swap properties and defer tax gains.

INSURANCE AGENT

- Seek an insurance agent familiar with rental properties.
- Check the insurance company's reputation for paying claims in a timely manner. (One way is to look it up in *Consumer Reports* or similar publications.)
- Make sure the maximum payouts on the insurance policy will cover all of your needs.
- Find out if the agent offers an umbrella policy that gives you additional insurance coverage that you can spread across your properties and covers other claims against you in the course of doing business.
- Follow the same principles as for finding a good attorney and accountant.

FINANCING SOURCES

- Find investor loan representatives from banks and/or mortgage companies or other investors who can be a source of funding for your business.
- Call well-known banks and ask to speak with the lending agent specializing in investor loans. That person may ask a few questions such as what type of investing you plan on doing (example answer: single-family homes, $80,000 to $150,000 range), then transfer you to the proper loan officer.
- Read ads in local newspapers (independent real estate papers, daily papers, or both) and look for ads from banks and mortgage companies directed at real estate investors. Our number one source for investor financing places an ad every month in the *Georgia Foreclosure Report* and other popular local investor newsletters.
- Check with established real estate investors and attorneys about good lending sources.

Friends and Family as Sources

Be cautious about getting loans from family and friends; it could become a big headache or worse. You risk losing control of the funds if the friend/family member questions decisions you make or withdraws support unexpectedly. The deal could also erode trust in your relationship or even split it apart. Therefore, if you work with friends and family as a source of funds, choose people you know and trust. Just as important, choose those who also know and trust you. Again, you will usually be better off in the long run self-financing your real estate transactions without the help of family and friends.

Accumulating Cash

Over time, we have been able to accumulate cash from our real estate business and use this cash to purchase more houses. This provides us with a lot of flexibility. We have been able to do this by keeping most of the cash in the business and building our business at a steady pace.

Remember: Cash Is King. This approach is consistent with our overall philosophy of steady and controlled growth.

Growing your Business Quickly

To jump in and grow your business quickly, you'll need to do a good job of finding investor money. Whomever you work with, aim to keep control so you can make sure your real estate investing program succeeds.

PROPERTY SOURCES

- Seek banks and mortgage companies specializing in marketing foreclosed (bank-owned) properties. The department in the bank or mortgage company is often called the Real Estate Owned or REO Department.
- Find the best REO agents. They often represent the banks and mortgage companies.
- Talk to other investors about prominent banks, mortgage companies, and REO agents in your area.

Banks and Mortgage Companies (REO Departments)

Call well-known lending companies and ask for the postforeclosure representatives or REO managers. Introduce yourself and give your geographic and price target markets (e.g., greater St. Louis, Missouri; single-family residential homes, minimum three bedrooms and two bathrooms; repaired and improved value falling in the $80,000 to $150,000 range). Ask to speak to REO managers for your specific geographic area. Find out how they manage sales. Can you work directly with them as an investor prior to listing the property, or must you work with their local REO agent(s)? If you must work with their local agents, ask for their contact information and introduce yourself to the agents. It is always advantageous to tell the agents which person at the bank referred you.

If asked, most of these lenders will give you monthly reports on foreclosure properties available. Remember, you are not the only one calling them so call back regularly, if possible every month, reintroduce your-

self, and again request current property listings. Sending a follow-up letter and setting up monthly correspondence is helpful, too. However,
once you have purchased your first property from this lender, you won't
need to keep reminding him or her who you are.

Focus your efforts on banks and mortgage companies that deal in
conventional loans. Because of additional government regulations that
apply to FHA and VA loans, the process for buying FHA and VA properties typically takes much longer and is less profitable.

As discussed earlier, look for a history of working well with investors
and a willingness to forgo agent commissions to work directly with you
when appropriate. This increases your opportunities for buying properties at a significant discount, because the banks or mortgage companies
don't have to pay a real estate agent's commission. Find out if the bank
or mortgage company is willing to finance the property you acquire, for
some of them will also have investor loans offered particularly for properties purchased from their own portfolios.

REO Agents

The top REO agents in your community have established good relationships with postforeclosure departments at banks and mortgage
companies. Some even have exclusive relationships; in other words, all
foreclosure business from certain banks or mortgage companies gets fil-
tered through these agents. Simply call agents around town and introduce yourself. Ask if their brokerage office handles any bank-owned
properties. If not, ask if they know which brokers do. Be sure to find out
which parts of the city they specialize in. If you find a match with your
target geographic region, be sure to let the agent know this. Often, agents
write *bank-owned* on their yard sign to draw more interest in the property.
After a while, you will notice the same agents' names appearing on signs
identifying bank-owned properties.

It's important to note if the agents have solid relationships with the
banks and mortgage companies they represent. (You will figure this
out for yourself over time.) They should have a strong portfolio of REO
properties, reflecting how much confidence the bank has in their work.
Determine if they have a pool of investors to draw from. Naturally, they
will try to sell properties first on the retail market, but if they can't, the

banks want them sold quickly and will eventually allow the REO agents to discount the properties for them. So those agents who have a pool of investors to contact will be able to move properties fast, and you want to establish yourself in this niche. Of interest, we have purchased approximately 80 percent of our properties from about five key contacts. It's our 80/20 rule: we get 80 percent of our properties from 20 percent of our key contacts. We have come to trust these people, and they now know which properties arriving in their portfolio are right for us.

CONTRACTORS/REPAIR PEOPLE

- Source two or three good contractors who do solid home repairs cost-effectively.
- To find good repair people, ask other investors and REO agents. They already have repair crews they work with regularly, and many can recommend reliable ones.
- For any contractors referred to you, check out the quality of their work and pricing practices. Also, determine their record for delivering on time; contractors can be notorious for overcommitting their resources and failing to stay on schedule. Their lateness costs you money, so do your best to get your project on the top of their priority list. Ideally, your contractor will advise you of all reasonable options. You can always expect changes as a job moves forward, but keep your antenna up for a contractor squeezing more expenses out of the job than necessary. The less handy you are and the less you check up on contractors, the more opportunity a contractor has to abuse you.

Hiring Small Contractors

We prefer hiring small contracting companies that do most (about 75 percent) of their own repairs rather than subcontracting the job to different specialists. We work with small contracting companies because they typically have lower overhead than larger contractors do and they tend to be more flexible. We prefer to have one main contractor per house. It is simply too difficult for us to manage four or five teams of workers simultaneously on the job site, and the specialists inevitably get in each other's way. Also, you want the job to be considered significant to the primary contractor; if you divide the pie too many ways, just one piece may not be worth a contractor's extra attention. The biggest downside of working with small contractors is they can't always get to our projects as soon as we would like. We try to minimize delays by talking to the contractor *before* scheduling the closing date. After all, when contractors can't do repairs right away, we have holding costs while no rent money is coming in. That's why it's important to plan ahead and have reliable contractors on your real estate team.

Contractor Loyalty

In the past six years, we have given about 90 percent of our work to two contractors. On the other hand, we've had our share of contractors we wouldn't use again. Our two primary contractors know our business and our pricing needs. They have repeatedly treated us fairly. Once you find a contractor with fair prices, dependability, and honesty, nurture that relationship. One way is by being fair (even generous) with bonuses when jobs are completed on time and at holidays. By showing appreciation, we let our contractors know we view their work as special, and in return we expect our jobs and needs to be a priority for them.

OUR PHILOSOPHY

Carefully identify and add the right numbers to your real estate team.

In every interaction with the people on your team, be straightforward, honest, fair, and reasonable. When you apply the basic principles of good relationships, you stand a good chance of developing a strong, reliable real estate team.

We believe in openly appreciating a job well done. This might take the form of a monetary bonus, a gift during the December holiday season, or a thank-you note. Even a verbal "thank-you" goes a long way. For example, one real estate agent has sold us one or two properties a year for the past five years. To show appreciation, we treat him to a special lunch in one of the finest restaurants in Atlanta at the end of every year. In addition to showing our appreciation, the lunch allows us to solidify our relationship. At one of our last lunches, he told us that we're first on his call list for northern Atlanta properties. He said he likes working with us because "Our word is golden" and our deals make him look good with the bank.

By treating your team members right and regularly showing thanks, you improve your odds of moving to the top of their lists. Besides simply being the right way to treat people, the relationships you build now will likely make a big financial difference in your rewards over the years.

In addition, leaving a positive impression on others has had a powerful boomerang effect. Here's a great example of this. We worked with one contractor whose own house accidentally burned down. When we heard about this tragedy, we made sure his family had gift certificates to restaurants to help cover meals, and we advanced him money against future work for us. The effect on our bottom line was negligible, but these actions allowed him to stay afloat—both for his family in the short-term and for us in the long run. We felt we helped him a reasonable amount, but he's never forgotten the kindness we showed during his hour of need. Since then, he has gone beyond expectations for us many times, and it's made a big difference in our relationship.

We treat our real estate team the way we try to treat everyone in our life—with respect. It's amazing how, when we treat people right, they continue to make a big difference by coming through for us again and again. The best part—everyone feels good in the process.

5

MONEY FOR PURCHASING YOUR HOMES

How much cash do you need to get started? How do you get a loan? How do you get the best bang for your dollar? What about your credit? This chapter answers these questions and others about financing your real estate investments.

CASH VERSUS FINANCING

We are living proof that you don't need a lot of money to get into this business, provided you start slowly. We've found many ways to make our cash go further and maximize our financing options. Our approach is to put as little cash into the home and spread out the payoff on the loan as long as possible (often 30 years). We try to do this without having to pay significantly more for the loan in the form of high interest rates, origination fees, mortgage insurance premiums, and other costs. This balancing act must be analyzed for each new loan.

If you're new to real estate investing, it's important to realize it takes time for your confidence and familiarity with the process to grow. It did for us also. And we survived the early 1990s, when the lending industry was reeling from its losses after the savings and loan scandals of the late

1980s. Because of the scandals, lending institutions tightened up their requirements for loans, making them hard to obtain. In addition, the terms for the investor loans weren't nearly as attractive as present-day investor loans. This fact alone affected our growth. Today, investor loans are much easier to find at much better interest rates than in the early 1990s.

There's no guarantee the economy won't return to the similar risk-adverse environment we experienced then. However, we believe the model described in this book works well even in a down economy. You may have to do more groundwork and grow more slowly than you'd like, but we have proved that it works.

Our advice: Start saving your money to buy real estate, and spend time learning what's going on in the real estate financing marketplace.

MONEY NEEDED WHEN PURCHASING A HOME

Several money factors must be understood when you purchase a home. Take time to understand what they are and determine how you should pay for them: cash, financing, or seller pays. The following are six important money factors:

1. *Down payment.* Typically 10 to 20 percent of sales price (e.g., $10,000 on a $100,000 home), usually paid with cash out of your pocket
2. *Closing costs on a loan.* Typically 2 to 3 percent of sales price (e.g., $2000 on a $100,000 home), which often can be paid by the seller or financed into the loan
3. *Repairs and improvements.* Can range from zero to $50,000 but usually fall in the $2,000 to $20,000 range and sometimes can be paid by the seller or financed into the loan
4. *Utility bills (electric, gas, water, etc.) prior to house being lease/purchased.* Typically $100 to $1,000 and paid with cash out of your pocket (after you lease/purchase the home, paid by the tenant)
5. *Advertising and marketing.* Typically $100 to $1,000 and paid with cash out of your pocket

6. *Mortgage payments prior to house being lease/purchased.* Typically $500 to $3,000 and paid with cash out of your pocket (after you lease/purchase the home, covered by your monthly rent)

Depending on how you structure your offer, you can require the seller to pay the closing costs and even the repairs. However, if you ask for too much, the deal can go south or may require setting up escrow accounts. So keep requests to a minimum, because you don't want these negotiations to tie up or even kill the sale.

R e a l - L i f e   E x a m p l e

During our early years, we looked at every possible means to minimize our cash outlay when making our offers. One time, we made an offer on a house needing about $10,000 in obvious repairs. Our offer was for approximately $100,000, with seller paying closing costs and contributing $10,000 toward repairs and improvements. The deal was contingent on our obtaining financing.

The offer we made netted out best for the seller and was accepted. However, we had two issues/problems with this transaction. First, when we went to get our loan, the particular lender had a problem with the large contribution toward repairs. The lender also questioned the "means" with which the contributions would be made. (When applying for investment loans, the investor usually must qualify for the loan based on overall income and financial picture, as well as have the necessary cash *not* to require contributions from the seller to purchase the house.) Anything suggesting an excessive contribution can raise a red flag for the lender.

We had to do one thing to satisfy the lender and complete this deal; we agreed that the seller's repair contribution check would go directly to our contractor. Most contractors require start-up money anyway and, as mentioned earlier, we know our contractors well and give them repeat business. For us, there was little risk of our contractor receiving a large, up-front payment and then leaving town for a pleasure trip. So the lender was satisfied that the seller's contribution would go toward the home repairs as the contract dictated, not as a financial supplement for the down payment. This arrangement allowed us to acquire the house.

Note: What can be a problem with one lender is often a complete nonissue with another. It is amazing how loan packages can vary, so be sure to discuss parameters with your lender or mortgage broker in advance. That way, you can minimize surprises once you have a contract on a house or are already closing the loan.

A *n o t h e r* **R** *e a l - L i f e* **E** *x a m p l e*

In a similar deal, we ran into a problem with the seller. The seller was fine with where our offer netted out (purchase price minus repair money given to us) but said there were simply too many contingencies attached to it. The seller saw our offer as a "cash-poor offer," which essentially it was (that is, at every corner we were asking the seller to contribute cash). We also had added a contingency about our securing financing. The seller felt (rightly so) that we might have problems qualifying for an investor loan with such a large seller contribution toward repairs. Therefore, we agreed to lower the seller's repair contribution from $10,000 to $3,000; in return, the purchase price was lowered $7,000. The net effect was this property required additional cash from our pockets for repairs of about $6,300 ($7,000 less the 10 percent we saved on down payment), but we did complete the deal with no further issues. We had the additional $6,300 available because we were trying to use as little cash as possible on this transaction. If we did not have the necessary cash, we still could have purchased this house using one of the creative loan tools described later in this chapter, but the terms on the loan would not have been nearly as attractive.

CASH ON HAND

Assess the cash you have on hand. Also, assess whether you have enough to cover all the key costs (described earlier) for a potential purchase. Pick a target, such as a $100,000 acquisition price on a house, with an available investor loan requiring 10 percent down payment, seller paying closing costs, minimal repairs, and so on. In our case, from the very beginning, we knew exactly what our cash limits were before we bought any house. Also, if you have a partner, determine which partner contributes how much to this venture. We've always contributed 50-50.

LOAN FINANCING OPTIONS

Educate yourself about the array of investor loans available. Shop around for the best interest rates and terms so you know the requirements of different lenders. That way, you'll also know how much cash you'll need to complete deals.

Below is some general information you'll uncover in your research. Understand this well, for this affects how you should structure your deals.

Down Payment, Term, and Interest Rate

Investor loans can be quite varied. Generally, though, they require a minimum 10 percent down payment on the purchase price of the house and a slightly higher interest rate than for loans for owner-occupied homes. Also, some investor loans have a lower interest rate in exchange for a higher percentage down payment. You will also find that longer-term loans typically carry a higher interest rate (e.g., 15-year loans usually carry lower interest rates than 30-year loans). But the trade-off is usually a lower monthly payment because the higher interest rate is spread over a longer period.

We often obtain 30-year loans even though they carry a slightly higher interest rate than 15-year loans. The monthly mortgage payment is usually 25 to 33 percent lower than that of a 15-year loan, making our monthly cash flow significantly higher (often more than 25 to 33 percent greater than the monthly rent). Additionally, because you're in the lease/purchase business and not the pure rental business, there's a reasonable chance your home will sell in the next few years, too soon to have any impact on the principal of your loan. Most of the mortgage payments during the first few years are assigned to pay off the interest, not the principal.

Origination Fees, Document Preparation Fees, and More

Banks and mortgage companies often make a lot of their money from these fees. For example, the origination fee is simply the fee they charge for giving you the loan. Typically, the lower the down payment, the better the interest rate, or the longer the term, the higher the fees. So check around and compare. These fees are sometimes negotiable.

Mortgage Insurance

Most investor loans are brokered by the federal government with mandates that those loans with less than 20 percent down payment (or equity in the property below 20 percent) carry private mortgage insurance, or PMI. This insurance provides the lender with financial recourse in case the borrower falls delinquent and defaults on the loan. PMI is relatively expensive: you'll pay approximately $75 to $300 a month for a home valued between $100,000 and $300,000 (PMI comes to 5 to 10 percent of your total mortgage payment). This adds ups to a significant amount over the life of the loan. Therefore, to avoid paying PMI, put down 20 percent. If you don't have an additional 10 percent to put down on a loan, then after the loan has matured—12 months into the loan—get the home reappraised. If the appraiser shows 20 percent or more equity in the property, the lender is required to remove the PMI portion of your mortgage payment.

With our program, we usually purchase properties at a 10 to 20 percent discount and put down 10 percent. So in a stable market, we have never had any problems removing PMI, and neither should you. Your only cost to do this is the price of the appraisal. *Make a note* to contact each one of your lenders about PMI removal once you have made 12 months of payments on the loan.

When we first started, we chose to tie up as little of our cash as possible, so we often put down less than 20 percent, the least down we could get away with while still securing fair terms (market-level interest rate). We recommend researching your options and determining how fast you want to grow. Then look at a complete picture and make decisions on how to spend your cash wisely.

Creative Loan Packages

Many creative loan packages are available to investors today that did not exist five or ten years ago. For example, say you acquire a house worth $100,000 for $40,000 and it needs $30,000 in repairs. You put down cash for 10 percent of the $40,000 purchase price and finance the balance at 7 percent. Then you take out a loan at 8.5 percent interest to cover $30,000 in repairs and improvements. On the upside, you use a minimum amount of cash ($4,000) to make this purchase, so it doesn't draw down your cash reserves. On the downside, borrowing funds at higher interest rates (the 8.5 percent on the repairs and improvements portion) increases your overall monthly outlay and, therefore, reduces your monthly cash flow.

Everything in real estate boils down to a trade-off. Therefore, you need to determine how much this project is worth to you and how you will benefit in the long run.

Preparing Credit Information for the Loan

Well in advance of your first purchase (and then at least once a year after that), obtain a copy of your credit report from a credit-reporting agency. You can obtain credit reports from Equifax <www.equifax.com>, Experion <www.experion.com>, and TransUnion <www.transunion.com>, sometimes even free of charge. Get familiar with your report and determine if you can improve your credit record. To secure investor loans with minimal hassles and reasonable terms, you'll need a credit report with few blemishes. If you're not sure what constitutes a blemish, invest a few dollars and visit a credit counselor with a copy of your credit report in hand.

Once you have an approved offer, things will move fast. The month you may have between acceptance of your offer and the closing on the sale of the home will seem like only a matter of days. Carefully organize your documents so they're ready. Be sure to include:

- W2s (from the last one or two years)
- Pay stubs (from day jobs for the last month or two)
- Copies of bank statements (for the last 2 to 12 months)
- Copies of tax returns (for the last two or three years)
- Copies of stocks and bonds
- Records of debts and obligations
- Other relevant financial information

Good Faith Estimate

After you've selected your financing source, the bank or mortgage company should prepare a good faith estimate for you. They will do this shortly after you lock in your loan and well in advance of the closing.

A good faith estimate itemizes all costs *before* closing so there are no surprises at the time of the closing. Be sure to read this document carefully. For example, make sure you understand how much the loan origination fee is. Also, review how different down payment percentages and loan durations affect the interest rate on the loan and, ultimately, your monthly mortgage payment.

Avoid Prepayment Penalties

Check to make sure your bank or mortgage company does *not* include a prepayment penalty. This is a fee for paying off the loan before it comes due and provides extra profit for the lending company. Borrowers can be unaware that this prepayment penalty exists, because it doesn't always show up in a good faith estimate. As an investor, you likely want to pay off your mortgage faster than is scheduled, and you don't want to incur any penalty for doing so. Therefore, make sure you specifically ask about prepayment penalties. If the terms on the loan specify a prepayment penalty, you should probably not use that loan because most don't require it. Seek alternative financing instead, and avoid paying the lender thousands of dollars unnecessarily. A good mortgage broker offering a varied portfolio of investor loans will understand this and should have a number of reasonable financing options for you without any prepayment penalties.

Using the Seller (Bank) as the Lender (Bank)

Determine if the same bank that is selling you the property will also finance your purchase of it. These banks often have an incentive to offer loans because (a) it's their core business and (b) it allows them to control the closing process and get the property off their books faster. At times, they even offer more favorable closing terms.

However, you can't count on these factors to be true. Most banks are big companies. The prime responsibilities of the REO department (moving properties) are different than those of the loan department (lending money), and often these two areas aren't in sync with each other. So have alternative sources lined up. Indeed, other lenders might give you better terms. Shop around, know your available financing options, and keep your contacts alive.

THREE-PHASE EVOLUTION FOR USING MONEY WISELY

In the early years, we chose to invest as little of our cash as possible in our real estate business, so we worked with low down payments and borrowed most of the funds. We even paid some extra costs to keep as much cash as we could in the bank and buy more homes. Gradually, we began to accumulate more cash from our real estate business and put more cash into the purchase to get better terms.

The following three phases describe our evolution, which may also work well for you.

Phase One—Minimizing Cash Expenditures

When we started, we would obtain loans with the minimum possible down payment, usually 10 percent. We would have to pay PMI on the loan, but after a year, we would reappraise the property, and it would always show 20 percent equity. We would then request the lender on the note to remove the PMI, thus lowering our mortgage payment 5 to 10 percent. We would always request that the seller pay the closing costs and usually some portion of the repair costs. If the seller did not pay the closing costs, we would examine investor loans that offered the option of the lender including the closing costs in the loan in exchange for a slightly higher interest rate (often between $\frac{1}{2}$ and 1 percentage point higher for loans in the mid-$100,000 range).

Phase Two—Simplifying Offers, Putting in More Cash

Later, we had enough money and enough confidence in our program to begin making more attractive offers (few contingencies). As our profits grew and we put them back into the business, we could cover our own costs. We were no longer as dependent on the seller contributing a large portion of cash toward repairs.

Also, as discussed earlier, a seller views contributions toward repairs, dependency on financing, and any other contingencies and strings attached to our offers as "something else that can go wrong with the sale." Consequently, the first significant change we made to our offers was to eliminate the repair and loan approval (financing contingency) require-ments, making our offers cleaner and simpler in the eyes of the seller. We did continue to ask the seller to pay closing costs, because contribut-ing to closing costs is very common and was not really complicating our offers in the eyes of sellers.

Phase Three—Buying with Cash and Borrowing to Refill the Coffers

Sellers love all-cash offers because they know you're serious and can move fast to close the deal. Even more important, as discussed above, you eliminate the contingency on financing, a huge consideration for the seller. You can put your offer in a special category in the seller's mind (simple, with little chance of the deal falling through).

Then, two months or so after you use your cash to purchase the home, you take out a loan against the property so you'll have cash on hand for your next purchase. In essence, this is a no-money-down pur-chase, although you needed access to the initial cash for a short period of time.

Here's an example of how it works. The asking price of a home is $50,000. The house needs $30,000 in repairs, but after they're complete, it should appraise for $100,000. So we buy the home—all cash—for $50,000 and spend $30,000 cash on repairs. Then we request an 80 per-cent investor loan (that is, 80 percent of the appraised value of $100,000, which comes to $80,000) and incur $3,000 in loan costs. We don't pay PMI because we have 20 percent equity in the property, plus we get a more favorable rate as our equity percentage is 20 percent rather than the 10 percent in phases one and two. Sometimes, we even walk away from the refinancing with an extra few thousand dollars in cash. Then, with this property now comfortably refinanced, we're able to put the cash to work again with our next purchase.

Phase three shows how we've been able to self-fund our real estate investment business. This approach maximizes the loans available be-cause it allows us to negotiate the best rates and avoid paying PMI, thus improving our monthly cash flow. When you have enough cash to do so, we suggest delaying refinancing until after you have lease/purchased the property. You may save on financing costs in those instances where you advertise lease/purchase but actually consider selling the home to someone interested in purchasing rather than lease/purchasing. If we receive an acceptable offer, we take it and the immediate profit, then put it right back into our business. We have just flipped this property—purchasing, repairing, and improving it, and selling for immediate profit. If we had obtained a loan upon acquisition, we would have paid several thousand dollars in financing costs for a note, which we would have used for maybe two to three months. But by purchasing the home entirely with cash, if we flip a property now and then, we make additional profit with the difference between what our loan costs would have been and any interest expense incurred for the use of the cash for two to three months.

We recommend you become experienced and confident in the process before considering self-funded, all-cash purchasing. By the time we arrived at phase three, we had attained a high level of comfort. We had proven that the formula works over and over, so we did not view allocating a large amount of cash as a significant risk. We also had made and accumulated enough cash from our real estate business so that these outlays did not significantly impact our personal finances.

OUR PHILOSOPHY

As we noted earlier, both of us loved playing Monopoly as kids. Absolutely loved it. We always wanted to collect properties, houses, and hotels and make money on them. Although Monopoly is a game, its reliance on acquiring properties and houses to build wealth is based in reality. Which other investment vehicle gives an investor an opportunity to take $10,000 and acquire an asset of $100,000? That means you don't have to pour your entire life's savings into real estate to start making money.

Our philosophy has been to build slowly, without overextending ourselves and relying entirely on self-financing (no outside investors) for our growth. Admittedly, much of that approach stemmed from the fact that, when we began our business, we only desired an income supplement to our day jobs, nothing more. By the time those goals changed, enough of our properties had sold over time to provide us with options we never dreamed of just five or ten years earlier.

After reading this book, we recommend you, too, take a good look at your available finances and overall goals when deciding how fast (or how slowly) you wish to grow your real estate business.

6

FINDING GOOD HOMES

What properties are you looking for? Where do you find the good deals? How do you know a good deal when you see one? How do you get good deals on properties without taking advantage of distressed sellers? This chapter lets you in on how to find good homes to buy.

DISTRESSED PROPERTIES THAT GO BACK TO LENDERS

To find good deals on properties, we have read many books, talked to countless investors, and purchased properties in a variety of ways. However, over time, we have learned that most of the good deals that fit our model are distressed properties that have gone back to the lender (bank or mortgage company) after foreclosure.

Although this isn't the only way we purchase properties, we have found it to be the best vehicle on a comparative and profitable basis. It allows us to purchase residential real estate without taking advantage of distressed sellers because the sellers, who are lenders (unlike many families we've heard about), understand *why* they are selling at a discount—

it's a function of their business. You may be asking yourself, shouldn't lenders be getting the best deal on home property sales—better than most people who are selling properties? Often, the answer is no for the following reasons.

Lending practices in America have relaxed considerably since the mid '90s on residential real estate, both for homeowner loans and investor loans. That means many families and investors who, years ago, did not have ample credit or down payment or both are now able to buy homes. However, because these people are usually stretched to their limit, many are unable to maintain their mortgage obligations if a financial crisis arises (e.g., lost job, sick family member, poor financial management, etc.). As a consequence, the foreclosure rate today on single-family homes is as high as it's ever been.

Further, most of these properties are going back to the banks that made the loan. This is because purchasing foreclosures on the courthouse steps (discussed later in this chapter) is a highly risky proposition. There's little, if any, time to inspect the homes, identify and research all liens associated with the property, and so on. Also, the lender's loan balance for these types of properties is usually close to the value of the house, because relaxed loan requirements have resulted in smaller down payments, and these foreclosures tend to happen in the first few years of the loan when the balance is still high. In addition, foreclosed properties often need significant repairs because the homeowners didn't have the money to keep up the home properly, or they may have even taken their frustration out on the home.

The postforeclosure departments of these lenders are now faced with the task of disposing of these properties, called *post foreclosures*. Postforeclosure departments are commonly referred to as REO (Real Estate Owned) departments.

As you know, banks and mortgage companies are in the business of lending money, not managing or selling properties. Each foreclosed property costs the company money in repairs, utilities, taxes, insurance, maintenance, and real estate agent commissions. Even more critical to lenders is that they are held back from doing their core business, because their money is tied up in homes and not collecting interest. Therefore, REO managers want to move delinquent properties out of their portfolios quickly—often selling these properties at steep discounts.

In addition to discounts, postforeclosure properties have at least three other advantages over properties you could buy on the courthouse steps. The banks usually (1) remove any title problems, tax liens, builders' liens, etc., (2) give the buyer ample time to inspect the property, and (3) throw in other goodies (repair money, closing costs, in-house investor loans, etc.). That's why our program concentrates on finding distressed properties that go back to banks and mortgage companies.

SINGLE-FAMILY HOMES IN MIDDLE-INCOME NEIGHBORHOODS

Single-family homes in middle-income neighborhoods work best for our business model because we use a lease/purchase method to sell most of our homes. Over time, we have found that middle-income people tend to make the best lease/purchase candidates and single-family homes tend to be the easiest to lease/purchase.

Most middle-income people dream of owning a home and often have the financial means to do so (or can eventually, once they've saved up the down payment or cleaned up their credit). But in our experience, prospective low-income homebuyers often lack the stability, funds, and conviction needed to purchase a home. This is why many homes in lower-income neighborhoods tend to be for rent.

By contrast, although upper-income prospective homeowners want to and can own a home, they're usually too wealthy and stable to need a lease/purchase program in the first place. In our experience, if an investor purchases an upper-income property, it takes longer to find the right lease/purchaser because the higher sales price reduces the pool of qualified buyers. That means the holding costs (number of months you have to make the mortgage payment, utilities, etc.) without any cash flowing in on the property from a tenant will be much higher (longer time multiplied by bigger monthly mortgage payments, utility bills, etc.). All income levels considered, that leaves middle-income people as the best match for our lease/purchase program.

We have also found that single-family homes in middle-income neighborhoods tend to be the most stable residential real estate investment and work best with our lease/purchase model. While condos, duplexes, and other variations to the single-family residential home may present extraordinary opportunities from time to time, we shy away from them because, in down economic times, these types of properties tend to be far less stable and devalue more than single-family homes. The same can be said for single-family residential homes in both lower-income and upper-income neighborhoods.

Again, because our model is designed for the long haul, we avoid short-term (and often short-lived) trends. That's why we stick with what we know best—single-family homes in middle-income neighborhoods.

WHAT TO LOOK FOR IN AN INVESTMENT HOME

Rarely do we come across two homes that are exactly alike. Two houses could even have the same floor plan but have different wall and floor coverings and other features. One could be on a hill while the other sits on a flat lot.

When considering homes to buy for investments, we look for standard items such as three bedrooms, two bathrooms, a one-car or two-car garage, a flat lot, standard floor plan, nice yard, etc. That being said, we are willing to deviate from our standard criteria, if and only if the deal is attractive enough to offset any home's particular deficiency (discussed below in "Valuing the Property"). However, what we don't deviate from is our single family homes in middle-income neighborhoods model.

To get a feel for a community, real estate valuations, trends, and differences between homes, we recommend initially practicing on one or two neighborhoods. Get to understand price difference as a function of extra bedrooms, bathrooms, and larger garages, as well as the value of a basement, larger lot, flat lot, pool, and so on. This helps considerably when coming across distressed properties in other stable middle-income neighborhoods you may not be as familiar with. Again, lenders loan money and take back distressed properties from all over the community, so get comfortable with determining the value of a home regardless of the neighborhood.

R *e a l - L i f e* E *x a m p l e*

We looked at a home in a solid, middle-income neighborhood in Atlanta. A hilly neighborhood gave many of the homes sloped and semifunctional lots. The property we were considering was on unquestionably the worst lot in the neighborhood. The front yard and driveway had about a 45-degree slope (this is not an exaggeration) and no functional backyard. As if this was not bad enough, the front yard was unkempt and suffered from serious soil erosion. A real eyesore.

Not surprisingly, its seller (a bank-owned property marketed by a local REO agent) was having a lot of difficulty finding buyers for this home. We were able to purchase it, but at an exceptionally large discount. In our offer, we played up the poor lot and appearance of the home for all it was worth. We deviated from our standards of what features we like in a home, but with a discount justifying the deviation. However, we did *not* deviate from buying single-family homes in a middle-income neighborhood.

There's a happy ending to this story. We fixed up the property and, because we got such a good deal upon acquisition and anticipated losing some good candidates due to the driveway, we were able to offer great terms under our lease/purchase program. When it came time to show the property, Andy had lined up ten appointments for our first Sunday showing. While he waited in the house and looked down the street, he watched several of his appointments drive up, take one look at the hill, and drive off without even coming in.

Eventually, though, we found lease/purchasers who truly appreciated our great terms (and the house). That family has been living there for over three years. We had to offer exceptionally attractive terms, such as a rent payment $200 lower than on a comparable home in the neighborhood on a good lot. Because we had anticipated this, our offer to the bank factored in all of the negatives associated with this home. The key was being able to determine its appropriate value and take action accordingly.

THE POTENTIAL INVESTMENT HOME CHECKLIST

Figure 6.1 is an example of a form you can use when you view a potential investment home. By using a form like this, you can more systematically do a thorough viewing of the home and neighborhood and assessment of the investment.

FIGURE 6.1 *Investment Home Checklist*

Date Property Seen _10_ | _13_ | _03_

Address _111 Denny Way_____ Price _$100,000_ Down Pmt. _$10,000_

BR _3_ BA _2_ GAR _2_ Prob. Rent _$995_____

Seller _Marie Bank_____ Phone _123-456-7890_

Age _10_ yrs. Neighborhood _stable, nice_____ 1- or 2-story _2_____ Driveway _flat_

Exterior: Roof _good_____ Landscape _good_____ Paint _bad_____ Trees _good_____

Front Yard _bad grass____ Backyard _bad grass_____ Fenced _no_____

Porch _yes___ Patio _yes____ Deck _yes____ Shed _no_____ Other _hilly_

Den: Fireplace _yes___ Walls _needs paint_ Carpet _good___ Ceiling _good___

Size _medium___ OH Light _yes_____ Ceiling Fan _no____ Other _no_____

Dining Room: Attached _no_____ Walls _needs paint_ Carpet _old____ Ceiling _good___

Size _medium___ OH Light _yes_____ Ceiling Fan _no____ Other _no_____

Kitchen: Size _large___ Walls _good_____ Floor _tile_____ Stove/Dish./Fridge _y/y/y_

Pantry _medium___ Cabinets _many____ Ceiling _good____ Other _island_

Garage: Size _oversize_ Opener _yes_____ Shelves _yes_____ Other _bike rack_

Hallway: Walls _good___ Carpet _old____ Linen Closet _yes___ Other _no_____

Laundry Room: Location _1st floor_ Size _medium_____ Other _extra closet_____

Master Bedroom: Size _large___ Walls _good_____ Carpet _good____ Ceiling _good___

Closet _large___ OH Light _yes____ Ceiling Fan _yes___ Other _no_____

1st Bedroom: Size _medium___ Walls _good___ Carpet _old_____ Ceiling _good___

Closet _medium___ OH Light _yes____ Ceiling Fan _no_____ Other _no_____

2nd Bedroom: Size _small__ Walls _good____ Carpet _old____ Ceiling _good___

Master Bath: Size _large___ Walls _good___ Floor _good___ Pressure _good___ Other _tub_

Hall Bath: Size _medium___ Walls _good___ Floor _old____ Pressure _good___ Other _2 sinks_

Rentals in Neighborhood:

Address _222 Dennis St._____ Phone _123-4567_ Size _3/2/2_ Rent _1,000_ Sec. Dep. _1,000_

Address _333 Danielle Rd._____ Phone _234-5678_ Size _4/2/2_ Rent _1,300_ Sec. Dep. _1,000_

Address _444 David Ave._____ Phone _345-6789_ Size _4/2/1_ Rent _1,000_ Sec. Dep. _1,000_

For Sale in Neighborhood:

Address _555 Diana Ln._____ Phone _456-7890_ Size _4/2/2_ Price _110,000_ Terms _by owner_

Address _666 Brian Cir._____ Phone _567-8901_ Size _3/2/2_ Price _100,000_ Terms _moving_

Address _777 Marcy Pl._____ Phone _678-9012_ Size _3/2/2_ Price _100,000_ Terms _none_

VALUING THE PROPERTY

Get Comps

The term *comps* is short for comparables, which are data sheets describing properties for sale and already sold in the same area. Usually we only review comps that are less than 12 months old because we want the most current information possible. If very few comps exist on a neighborhood, we sometimes refer as far back as 18 months.

Comps can be obtained from:

- Real estate agents who subscribe to a local real estate listing service (e.g., the Multiple Listing Service or MLS)
- Internet services such as Lexis/Nexis (costs about $100/month)
- Local newspaper Web sites (e.g., the *Atlanta Journal Constitution* has free comps of recent sales at <www.ajc.com>)
- Local tax offices
- Local real estate newsletters

Additionally, some neighborhoods may only yield two or three comps that are on target for you. To glean more information, go outside of the neighborhood to see comparable values, talk to several agents who work in the area, and gather various viewpoints. All this information will help you to assess the true value of a property.

Analyze Comps Carefully

Compare the values of houses that are, indeed, comparable. That means if a three-bedroom house has a finished basement and a similar three-bedroom house doesn't, they are not perfectly comparable properties. You don't want to compare an "apple to an orange." Therefore, you'll have to adjust your analysis to make it an apple-to-apple comparison. It may be that finished basements in that subdivision add approximately $15,000 in value to comparable properties without finished basements. If this is the case, then factor in $15,000, so that the data on the comparable sale of the home with a finished basement can help in your analysis.

Often you can determine these price adjustments by comparing several comps (e.g., comparing two comps with finished basements and two without could reveal a consistent $15,000 difference), but also call one or two agents with "For Sale" signs in the neighborhood to get even better information.

Read comps to identify increases or decreases in prices of properties. Get a feel for the overall values, plus any tendency for values to be inching up, inching down, or remaining stable. As you do apples-to-apples comparisons, you're able to determine fair market values (good purchase prices).

Again, the fresher the data the better. Four or 5 comps from the last year are more valuable than 10 or 15 comps that are older.

Drive the Neighborhood

Before you make any offers, get a good feel for the neighborhood. Do the other homeowners take good care of their homes? Are there many homes in the neighborhood in need of paint, new roofs, yard care? If so, this can tip you off to a potential problem on the horizon. If not, this is probably a good, stable neighborhood that will retain and increase its value.

While you drive around, pull flyers from "For Sale" signs to gather additional information about homes in the neighborhood. Also, take time to visit open houses (usually held on weekends) as part of your research. Homes having open houses typically don't sell at a discount. By visiting open houses, though, you'll get a feel for how people fix up their homes and which attributes stand out. Knowing this will help you immeasurably when factoring the costs of making improvements to the value of your property. Please note that we recommend open houses only from the standpoint of determining the value of a home you are considering purchasing. You're unlikely to get the good deals we discuss in this book by buying an open house property.

Research Plans for the Community

To find out about short-term and long-term plans for the neighborhood, read local newspapers and check the Internet. Talk to real estate agents with listings in the neighborhood (though they'll usually be biased because they need to talk up the neighborhood). Are highways, parks, retail stores, schools, etc., scheduled to be constructed? If so, how will they impact the neighborhood and its future property values? What are people in the area saying about these plans?

Remember, there's no substitute for staying on top of issues related to your property.

Determine the Going Rental Rates

It's important to understand the cash flow you'll get from the rent when you lease/purchase the property. This can be evaluated several ways. Check the neighborhood for "For Rent," "For Lease," or "For Lease/ Purchase" signs. If any homes are for rent in the neighborhood, call and find out about the rental amount, house size, and other particulars. You may even want to visit the property yourself to compare it to yours.

Also, check the local newspaper for homes for rent in the general vicinity. The paper may not list the particular subdivision, but you'll get a good feel for the rental rate for similar homes in the part of town you are evaluating.

UGLY AND AWFUL HOMES— OFTEN GREAT PURCHASES

You know them—the eyesores of the neighborhood. Like the home with the 45-degree sloping driveway, these houses have unattractive physical characteristics that detract from their full market value and are hard to sell. But to a real estate investor, these eyesores can be beautiful—and very profitable. So don't shy away from ugly and awful homes; be attracted to them.

Remember, we're often dealing with properties that have been foreclosed. In many cases, the world of the homeowner was collapsing, and often the lender has become (in the eyes of the homeowner) the hated landlord. Sadly, people in these tough situations often take out their rage on their homes: breaking windows, punching holes in walls, leaving trash everywhere, and so on. Other foreclosed homes have simply not been maintained properly due to the inadequate finances of the previous homeowner. No wonder they don't sell.

Interestingly, banks usually feel like they have too much money in the home already and are reluctant to spend any more on repairs or improvements. At the same time, when middle-income people are looking for houses, few consider buying a fixer-upper needing thousands (or tens of thousands) of dollars worth of work. This gives you a significant advantage when negotiating a purchase price on an ugly and awful home with a bank.

Remember that the bank has already put a lot of money into the property, and banks tend to dislike the renovation business. In fact, many banks, as a matter of policy, do virtually no repairs and upgrades. Some take care of basic cosmetic problems like carpet and paint, but we have yet to find a bank that does major renovations such as knocking out a wall to create a functional room, building a laundry room, repairing termite damage, landscaping, etc.

How Ugly and Awful Works

Here's how ugly and awful has worked for us. We go into a home and visualize what needs to be done to fix it up. Many times, what actually makes the home ugly and awful is simply cosmetic in nature—poor paint on the inside and out, old ratty carpeting, worn hardwood floors, weed-infested front yard, etc. Usually, these problems are easily remedied with one or two coats of paint, new carpet, refinished floors, basic landscaping, and so forth. When we know the home will need extensive work, we survey it with our contractor who gives us an estimate on costs for repairs and improvements. (See Chapter 9, "Fixing Up Your Homes.")

Remember, most homebuyers in your target neighborhood are looking for a house that's ready to move into—not a house to fix up—even if the repairs are cosmetic. That need creates a special opportunity for you.

On the other hand, some of the ugly and awful of a house may not be fixable. The home may have characteristics or attributes that are difficult and costly, if not impossible, to change (e.g., the architectural design, the lot size or layout, etc.).

The first home we bought together had a steeply sloping driveway—about 30 degrees. This particular lot was wooded, so with the slope and the trees, the home wasn't visible when driving by the lot. We factored these negatives into our offer and were able to get a substantial discount on the purchase. We then lease/purchased the property for a fair price, and the lease/purchasers bought it a few years later. To this particular family, the terms of our lease/purchase program were more important than the home itself (a factor detailed in Chapter 12, "Finding the Right Lease/Purchasers"). Because of the bigger-than-usual discount we got on the purchase of the property, we made a larger profit than usual. That's why we love the ugly and awful homes. Homes that others don't want are often most profitable for us. The bigger the eyesore, usually the more the profit.

Ugly and awful homes work for us for two primary reasons. First, as described above, unlike most people who won't purchase fixer-uppers in middle-income neighborhoods, we are willing and eager to fix up properties as long as we are compensated for our efforts. This works especially well for the repairs and improvements of a cosmetic nature. Second, as described in Chapter 11, "Marketing Your Homes," we use our lease/purchase format to market and eventually sell the property.

The key point to recognize here is that people tend to buy the home from us *more* for our financial terms (the lease/purchase terms) and *less* because of the actual home (the look and layout of the home). Indeed, people we attract into our lease/purchase program are happy simply to be able to own a home. The terms give them a reasonable chance to own a home in the near future, so they're willing to overlook certain unappealing attributes. That makes our approach different from how most sellers (and real estate agents) market homes for sale.

Over the years, the sellers and REO agents in our network have learned to count on our marketing program being different enough to override the negative characteristics of these properties. Many of our longtime contacts know that when they find a property in a nice neighborhood needing substantial renovations and standing out as an eyesore, they can call us for a quick and simple discounted sale.

See why we're not scared off by the ugly and awful?

Play the Waiting Game

Sometimes we play a waiting game with the bank that's holding the property. If the REO manager turns down our discounted offer, we wait one month, three months, or sometimes longer depending on the situation, to see if the property is still on the market. Then we make another offer, usually just resubmitting our original offer.

As you might expect, REO managers can get tired of holding on to properties as costs keep mounting, and (again) they typically don't like to invest large sums of money and time in renovating a property. They get to know they can call us later if they want to accept our offer.

Even more important, we stay on top of each possibility. In fact, one time we submitted the same offer sheet to the bank/seller several months in a row, changing only the date each time by crossing out the old one and writing in the new one. The REO manager finally accepted our original offer—six months after we made it.

Unique Detrimental Characteristics

From time to time, you will come across properties with negative attributes, like steep driveways, that are difficult to assess and value. If you choose to move forward with such a property, do so smartly. Pay close attention to every detail and discuss the pros and cons of deviating from the standards you've set.

As partners in this real estate business, we have tremendous respect for one another, although we think differently on many occasions. One way our partnership has worked well shows up when we find homes like this. We have learned that it makes a difference when the two of us are weighing the choices and making the decisions together. If you are investing on your own, then seek out advice from other respected professionals (investors, real estate agents), particularly when considering homes with unique detrimental characteristics. Be sure you feel comfortable that you're accounting for these characteristics with an appropriate and compensatory discount in your offer to the seller.

WORKING YOUR REAL ESTATE NETWORK

The following list contains some key ways to find good deals on properties.

- Working with REO agents
- Working with the REO departments at banks

- Referrals from members of our team
- Working with distressed sellers
- Other creative sources

Methods one and two make up our primary sources of properties. Again, REO stands for Real Estate Owned, which means that the home has been foreclosed on and is now owned by a lender (bank or mortgage company). Method three has also yielded some properties as our team members learn our business.

As noted earlier, foreclosures in the United States have been increasing in recent years and are likely to keep doing so. Relaxed government guidelines for loans have made it easier for many to qualify for a homeowner loan. Also, creative homeowner loan packages have made it easier to secure a homeowner loan for little or virtually no cash for the down payment. These terms have created a situation in which families, after two or three years, have little equity in their homes. Therefore, given rough financial times, a family has little incentive not to simply walk away from its mortgage obligation. Further, many Americans continue to live beyond their means, taking on more debt than their incomes can handle. Even when their income is adequate, many don't allow for a safety net for unexpected illness, job loss, or other emergencies.

All of these factors have led to a huge increase in foreclosures in our country. Couple that with banks not being in the business of managing, fixing up, or selling properties. Accordingly, if their properties do not produce retail revenue from a fairly quick sale, they will be discounted (often steeply); it is simply a matter of time. That's why we spend the majority of our time working with REO agents and REO departments.

Working with REO Agents

Working with REO agents—our most frequently used resource—has become easier over time. Some REO agents are skeptical of new, unproven investors and are hesitant to spend too much time and effort with them. As these specialized real estate agents have gotten to know us and our target geographic and price ranges, they call us when they have a property in their portfolio that's a match. In general, once we purchase two or three homes from an agent, that person has a good feel for what we do, and our relationship goes on autopilot. The best REO agents often have ties to a community, so we experience little turnover in our key contacts.

Working with REO Departments at Banks

Working with bank REO departments directly—our second most frequently used method—requires more time and energy than working with REO agents. Usually, the banks (and mortgage companies) are not local, so we rely on a phone relationship with our key contacts. To nurture these relationships, we need to call each REO manager on a regular basis (we try to do this monthly). They rarely call us, even after we've purchased a number of properties from them.

Additionally, because they work in corporate positions, often the relationship ends due to employee turnover and transfers. That means having to start from scratch with each new REO manager. Don't be shy; if you have a new contact and have done business with his or her bank in the past, don't hesitate to let your new contact know about it.

Purchasing directly from banks' REO departments is a profitable means of acquiring properties because it cuts out the middle man—the REO agent. However, working with this primary source of properties requires phone calls during the business day and considerably more effort than purchasing from local REO agents. In addition, some banks simply don't allow direct sales; they work exclusively through REO agents.

Referrals from Members of Our Team

Our real estate team has also proven to be a profitable source of properties for us. We have purchased a number of homes directly because our team members become additional eyes and ears in the community. In fact, our contractors have spotted a number of homes for us. That's why it's important to build a real estate team for yourself.

Other Creative Sources

Of course, there are other creative ways to find good homes, such as building relationships with non-REO agents. For example, we have pur-

Real-Life Example

One time, we actually bought a home right across the street from one we had just purchased. This happened because a neighbor saw renovations happening on the house we had just purchased, a real neighborhood eyesore. He walked over to talk with our contractor. He told the neighbor we were investors who are fair and reasonable people. As investors, we need to buy at a discount, but we don't use high pressure and can move quickly. Our contractor then gave him our phone number. He had to sell his house quickly, so he called us right away. We explained our discounting policy and after negotiating the details, we bought his house within two weeks of his walk across the street. Again, he paid no holding costs or commissions, we got a good deal on the property, and we gave our contractor an extra bonus, so everyone won.

Here's the icing on the cake: these two homes were purchased within a month of each other and were similar in style and interior. One of the families that responded to the ad on the first home became the family we selected for the second home, so our marketing costs on the second home were virtually zero.

chased a handful of properties from a particular agent at a large real estate firm that specializes in corporate relocations. The same principles described above for dealing with REO agents apply to corporate relocation specialists. We have also purchased a property from an auctioneer who specializes in pooling bank-owned properties and auctioning 30 or more at one time.

In fact, there are numerous creative sources we haven't pursued. Some investors have tried running ads in local newspapers or posting signs advertising the ability to purchase homes quickly. Others have driven around neighborhoods looking for homes in disrepair. Still others have followed the obituaries and contacted out-of-town relatives, making a quick sale offer to an out-of-town heir who may have absolutely no desire to deal with a normal listing process during a time of grieving.

There are hundreds of additional ways to secure a healthy profit margin in real estate, and there are also hundreds of books detailing these methods. Obviously, we favor our methods. They are simple, relationship oriented, and do not take advantage of others by promoting profit at another's expense. What's more, they're profitable.

AVOID TAKING ADVANTAGE OF DISTRESSED FAMILIES

Working with distressed sellers has not been our focus; in fact, it's been one we've tried to avoid. Again, we negotiate quite aggressively with REO managers and agents, but we take a passive approach with distressed homeowners because we don't want to take advantage of anyone in a dire situation. We only talk with distressed sellers if they come to us—we don't go looking for them.

It's our policy to explain our discount approach to distressed sellers up front. If they're not interested, we simply walk away. Many investors who deal with foreclosures make significant profits at the expense of dis-

---

R *e a l - L i f e* E *x a m p l e*

We once purchased a house that had sat vacant for five years and had never been on the market. The woman who owned the home had lived in a nursing home for the first few years, but the family just couldn't bear to sell the house they grew up in while she lived.

One of the real estate agents on our team was friendly with the woman's daughter, so the agent told her about us. The daughter also knew the house would need significant repairs and improvements before being properly marketed, and she didn't have the cash to do the work (nor did she want to take out a loan).

So we outlined the estimated cost of repair and improving the property to our real estate agent and set the discount we would need to make the deal attractive. We never submitted a written offer (this is a rare exception to our rule, which we will discuss later in the book), because the owner was an individual with emotional ties to the property and we didn't want to unduely pressure her. Essentially, we wanted her to know we were out there as a fallback option, if need be.

After several years of sitting on the property and paying annual taxes and monthly utilities, the daughter eventually called the agent and asked if we'd still be interested in buying the home. We were, and we purchased the property at a steeply discounted price.

That's how our network works. If you continue to build your real estate business, *wonderful opportunities will begin to come your way.* We continue to be amazed at how finding good deals continues to get easier in proportion to our growing network of contacts in the real estate field.

tressed sellers. Our rule is that we have no unsolicited contacts with people in tough circumstances; we only follow opportunities that come to us and (as described in the real-life example about the mother in a nursing home) never use high pressure or aggressive sales tactics. Again, when we deal with distressed sellers, which is rare, we are passive purchasers.

FORECLOSURE SALES ON THE COURTHOUSE STEPS

Many familiar with the foreclosure process will suggest purchasing at the foreclosure sale on the courthouse steps when certain properties become legally available for purchase. This method can also be profitable, but we have shied away from it for the following reasons.

- When purchasing properties on the courthouse steps, properties in most jurisdictions are subject to all attached liens—such as tax liens and contractor liens—and may also have significant title issues. Depending on the particular preforeclosure laws in your state, you generally have two to four weeks prior to the foreclosure sale to research and investigate the homes. Some companies purchase foreclosures on the courthouse steps at the monthly foreclosure auction as a full-time business. These companies generally have attorneys on hand who research the properties in detail for liens and other issues. On a positive note, all junior debts tend to be wiped out on the courthouse steps.
- Often, investors cannot get into a preforeclosure property to inspect it and put together a repair and improvement estimate. They have to go on the word of the bank as to the extent of repairs and improvement needed for the property. All purchases on the courthouse steps are "as is" with *no escape clauses*—buyer beware. As noted above, if you are purchasing in bulk, these risks or occasional misses are typically offset (assuming you are purchasing wisely). However, if you are purchasing a small number of homes this way, you may be incurring a lot of risk.
- Finally, purchasing on the courthouse steps usually requires tremendous amounts of cash. In most states, the successful bidder is obligated to pay for the property immediately (sometimes within 24 hours) in full—and ownership is transferred on the spot.

OUR PHILOSOPHY

Being able to focus on distressed foreclosed properties owned by banks and mortgage companies has made a big difference in our success, and the ugly and awful properties have made an even bigger impact on our profits. The key is to understand *how to find* good properties and then *how to recognize* a good deal when you find it.

In addition, everything you do is intertwined with the jobs and lives of others, and everyone on your real estate team can provide additional eyes and ears. This benefit comes to fruition after two or three years of continuous, systematic effort.

We hope this chapter has given you an appreciation of the importance of your real estate network (REO agents, non–REO agents, contractors, etc.) when it comes to bringing you real estate investment opportunities. As they continue to make a difference in finding properties, remember to make a difference for them by compensating them fairly for their efforts. We have had a lot of success over the years, and a lot of it has come from our hard work. Yet, without a doubt, we would not have found nearly as many good properties without the superb people who are part of our long-standing real estate network.

7

MAKING OFFERS
AND NEGOTIATING PURCHASES

When it's time to make an offer, how do you proceed? What are the key price points? How do you negotiate to close out the purchase of the property? This chapter explains our approach.

UNDERSTANDING KEY PRICE POINTS

Before you make an offer, you need to have a good understanding of the following two price points:

1. *Ceiling price.* The most you will pay to acquire the property
2. *Initial offer price.* The amount you first offer to get the negotiations off to a good start

To determine these two price points, it's critical to take into account the seller's asking price (the amount the seller is trying to sell the property for), the amount you think you can eventually sell or lease/purchase the property for, and the costs to acquire the property and fix it up into a condition comparable to others in the neighborhood.

Also, if the seller's asking price is the same or close to those of similar homes in the neighborhood, you may be wise to avoid wasting time evaluating the property. You likely won't get the discount you need to make this a good investment property.

The Ceiling Price—Key Variables

The ceiling price is the most you'd pay for the property. It is a combination of your investor discount *plus* key cost considerations.

Investor discount. Your investor discount is your profit and should be 10 to 20 percent off the fair market value of the property in "good condition." (See Chapter 6, "Finding Good Homes," on how to determine the fair market value.) The reason the investor discount assumes the house is in good condition to determine the amount—even if the property needs vast repairs and improvements—is that the ceiling price formula also includes compensation for you to bring the home to good condition (see the list of key cost considerations below). Usually, the more repairs and improvements that are needed for the home, the higher the investor discount you should secure. Be sure to get compensated more for the time and headaches associated with a home needing $20,000 in repairs; the hassle far exceeds that associated with a home in mint condition that is ready for lease/purchasers to move in.

Key cost considerations. The following are *key cost considerations* to help you establish your ceiling price.

- Repair and improvement costs (paint, new roof, flooring, etc.)
- Closing costs (attorney's fees, etc.)
- Finance costs (loan origination fees, etc.)
- Taxes and insurance costs
- Marketing costs (newspaper ads, signs, brochures, etc.)
- Utility costs prior to lease/purchasing the property (gas, electric, water, etc.)
- Mortgage payments or equity line costs (while fixing up the house and marketing it)
- Miscellaneous costs (always budget extra for surprises)

Calculating the Ceiling Price

Now that we've listed the variables that go into the ceiling price equation, let's use an example to illustrate how to calculate it.

Fair market value. Let's say you find a house that would sell for $100,000 in good condition. This is the fair market value of the property after all appropriate repairs and improvements have been completed. You've learned this by analyzing comparable properties in the neighborhood and completing the other steps discussed in Chapter 6, "Finding Good Homes."

Investor discount. This home needs a medium to high amount of repairs. You decide to go for the middle of the investor discount range of 10 to 20 percent and choose 15 percent. In this case, your investor discount is $15,000 (15 percent of the property's fair market value of $100,000).

Repair and improvement costs. After a walk-through with your contractor, you find the house probably needs a new roof, new paint inside and out, and much more, so your estimated repairs and improvement costs are $15,000. (See Chapter 9, "Fixing Up Your Homes.") Remember, there may be hidden problems that can be found only during a more rigorous inspection by your inspector or contractor, but that's why you have the protection clauses in your contract. (See Chapter 8, "The Real Estate Purchase Contract.")

Closing costs. You then talk to your real estate attorney. You learn that the closing costs (attorney's fees, etc.) in your area will probably be about $500. Realize that the lender who gives you the loan on your property actually gets to choose the attorney, and it might not be yours. However, closing costs in a particular community are often similar (within a couple of hundred dollars) from attorney to attorney. (See Chapter 5, "Money for Purchasing Your Homes.")

Finance costs. From your research, you also know that finance costs (loan origination fees, etc.) are approximately 2 percent of the loan amount; therefore they'll be about $2,000. (See Chapter 5, "Money for Purchasing Your Homes.")

Taxes and insurance costs. You then talk to a real estate agent who tells you that taxes in the neighborhood are around $500 a year for homes not occupied by the owner (no homestead exemption for you, the investor). You probably could also obtain this information from the county records, your local real estate agent's database, or an online database like Lexis/Nexis. Your insurance agent then tells you that the insurance cost for a $100,000 house in that area is around $200 a year for a rental dwelling (no owner-occupied discount for you, the investor). Therefore, your taxes and insurance costs total $700.

Marketing costs. You call the local newspaper and find out it costs $75 a week to advertise your home using a four-line ad. You estimate it will take you three weeks to find the right lease/purchaser ($75 times 3 equals $225). Add in another $25 for sign and flyer costs, and your total marketing costs are estimated at $250.

Holding costs (utility costs plus mortgage payments). You also determine the house will take five to six weeks to repair and add this to your estimated three weeks to get the home lease/purchased after it's repaired. (Remember, we estimated three weeks for marketing purposes.) You decide to calculate your holding costs (utilities—gas, electric, water, etc.) and mortgage payments (equity line payments) for a period of three months to be on the safe side. Your utility costs during your holding period are estimated to be $100/month or $300 total (3 times $100/month). When you contact your bank for the origination fee, you find out that a loan on a $75,000 house would have a monthly mortgage payment (principal and interest) of $500. (Note: $75,000 is probably more than you'd pay for this $100,000 home at fair market value, because you always buy at a discount and it needs repairs, but this is a worst-case estimate.) Your estimated mortgage payments during the holding period will be $1,000 (2 times $500/month because you pay interest in arrears for a new home, which essentially means you don't make a payment the first month). Therefore, your total holding costs are $1,300 (utility costs of $300 plus mortgage payments of $1,000).

Miscellaneous costs. In this case, you feel comfortable with 10 percent on top of the original $15,000 for repairs and improvement costs. Therefore, you decide to budget $1,500 in miscellaneous costs.

Final calculation. Now let's do the math.

Fair Market Value (in good condition)	**$100,000**
Investor Discount (15 percent)	($15,000)
Repairs and Improvements Costs	($15,000)
Closing Costs	($500)
Finance Costs	($2,000)
Taxes and Insurance Costs	($700)
Marketing Costs	($250)
Utility Costs	($300)
Mortgage Payments	($1,000)
Miscellaneous Costs	($1,500)
Total Costs	($21,250)
Ceiling Price	**$63,750**

To summarize: The fair market value of the property in good condition is estimated at $100,000. You decide an investor discount of 15 percent, or $15,000, is fair. All of your key cost considerations add up to $21,250. Therefore, your ceiling price (the maximum you should pay for this property) is $63,750.

Calculating the Initial Offer Price

Now that you know what your ceiling price is, you are ready to come up with an initial offer price. This price should be 10 to 25 percent below your ceiling price to give you some wiggle room in your negotiations. We call it the *wiggle room discount.*

Remember, your preferred home is often a distressed property, one needing lots of repairs and improvements and one that few people want to buy in its present condition. Banks rarely want to invest money fixing up a property, often not even to repair the basics (carpet and paint). Therefore, the more repairs and improvements the property needs, the bigger the wiggle room discount you can begin with in your negotiations.

First, consider the seller's asking price. The goal is to come in with an initial offer price that's as low as possible but still have your offer taken seriously—and possibly even accepted. Although you shouldn't be afraid of choosing an initial offer price that the seller doesn't take seriously, it's best to avoid this scenario so you can get the negotiations moving and get the home purchased.

Note that, though we discourage you from buying properties directly from families who own them, if you are considering it, be careful when you choose your initial offer price. When sellers also live in the houses, they tend to take the offers personally because of their emotional attachment to their homes. In fact, they may even get insulted and upset with your offer price. That's why we prefer to deal with lenders (banks and mortgage companies) who have no emotional attachment to the properties they own. The transaction is strictly business to them.

Asking price versus ceiling price. Let's go back to the example in which we established the ceiling price to be $63,750 for a home worth $100,000 after making all the appropriate repairs and improvements to put it into good condition.

The seller knows the house needs a lot of work, and the asking price is $75,000. You realize there's a gap of $11,250 between what the seller wants ($75,000) and the most you'll pay ($63,750). Again, your goal is to buy it at, or preferably below, your $63,750 ceiling price.

Wiggle room discount and potential initial offer price. As described above, you establish your initial offer price by subtracting your wiggle room discount of 10 to 25 percent off the ceiling price. Because this home needs a medium to high amount of repairs and improvements ($15,000 on a $100,000 home), your wiggle room discount should be closer to 25 percent than 10 percent. Therefore, you start with 20 percent or $12,750 (20 percent of $63,750) and make it $13,750, getting the potential initial offer price a nice round number of $55,000 ($68,750 ceiling price minus $13,750 wiggle room discount).

Initial offer price—red face test. Now you compare the $55,000 to the seller's asking price of $75,000 and decide if this will stand up to the "red face test"—will it be taken seriously? Often, the relationship you have established with your REO agent can pay dividends here. If you think this number will be taken seriously, then it becomes your actual initial offer price. If not, then adjust your initial offer price upward. Remember, you don't want to go above your ceiling price, *and* you want to give yourself a reasonable amount of wiggle room to negotiate in.

In this case, your initial offer price is $20,000 below what the seller's asking price is ($75,000 minus $55,000 potential initial offer price). Still, the home needs a lot of work to be in good condition, and you know few buyers are willing even to look at properties like this. In fact, for every buyer who looks at it, even fewer will be willing to repair and improve it. Because the seller also knows this, your $55,000 initial offer price should pass the red face test.

Once you have determined your ceiling price and initial offer price, you are ready to make your offer and proceed with the negotiations. Remember, your desired outcome during the negotiations is to arrive as close as possible to your initial offer price without exceeding your ceiling price.

THE NEGOTIATING PROCESS

There are many approaches to negotiating. The goal of this book is to show you our proven real estate investment process, not necessarily to show you how to negotiate well. Fortunately, you can read books and go to seminars to learn how to negotiate. We highly recommend that you find a negotiating style that works for you and get good at it. After five or six transactions, you'll settle into a style that becomes comfortable. However, no matter what style you use, always negotiate with integrity and respect.

Applying Ceiling Price and Initial Offer Price

The following illustrates how to apply the ceiling price and initial offer price in negotiations, continuing with our example. To recap, the house has a fair market value of $100,000 in good condition. After we do all the repairs and improvements, we are targeting a 15 percent investor discount (so we don't have more than $85,000 into the house, including our loan and cash out of our pocket). We have estimated that the key cost considerations (repairs, holding costs, utilities, etc.) are $21,250. Therefore, our ceiling price to make this deal work is $63,750.

We also looked at the seller's asking price of $75,000 and decided on an initial offer price of $55,000 (that includes an approximate 20 percent wiggle room discount). We feel comfortable the seller would take this offer seriously and might even accept it. Making this determination is *especially* important when working with banks and REO agents, because we don't want to be viewed as wasting people's time. Rather, we want to be viewed as reasonable and easy to work with.

We believe in starting with a reasonable initial offer price, not an outrageously low amount, because we don't want to establish a reputation as being lowballers (those who make ridiculously low offers and try to "steal" properties). We want to be in the real estate investment business for the long run.

During negotiations, we resist bumping up the price from the initial offer too quickly; doing so can negate the initial offer price and the reasoning behind it. That's why we present sensible reasons for our offers and move our number up slowly and cautiously. Most often, we bump up our counteroffers in increments of $1,000 to $5,000, depending on the situation. When we get to our ceiling price, we stick to our guns and rarely budge.

Presenting the initial offer. We present our initial offer price in a written contract—the real estate contract—with a cover letter justifying why our offer is lower (in this example, significantly lower) than the seller's asking price. The cover letter lists much of the same information we used in establishing our ceiling price. (See Chapter 8, "The Real Estate Purchase Contract.")

Responding to counteroffer(s). Almost always, the bank won't accept the initial offer and responds with a counteroffer. In our example, the

---

R *e a l - L i f e* **E** *x a m p l e*

An offer not taken seriously by the seller: After we bought a home at a very good price, we began advertising to find someone to lease/purchase it. In response to our ad, a man called and in a huffy, angry voice, said, "I put a bid on that house, and the agent never even returned my call." As we talked further, we found out that his offer was tens of thousands of dollars below ours. In this case, the seller did not take him seriously, not only because his offer was ridiculously low but also because he made it verbally, which is unprofessional. The moral of the story: always make your offers reasonable and put them in writing.

bank wants more than we offer and counters at $67,000. We have to stretch all of the counteroffers we make over our $13,750 wiggle room amount. Our next offer is at $60,000; the bank comes back asking for $65,000. We restate our reasons for arriving at our price, telling the bank we're willing to split the difference at $62,500. The bank accepts, and we have a contract to purchase a home at a price that's $1,250 below our ceiling price. Just because we're willing to go to $63,750 doesn't mean we have to end up there.

LEVERAGING RELATIONSHIPS WITH REO AGENTS

When you've developed a solid relationship with your REO agent, he or she can give you some hints about what a reasonable initial offer price might be and how to proceed in negotiations. Always qualify the information; remember, the REO agent's primary responsibility is to get maximum resale value for his or her client, the bank. However, sometimes sharing certain information with you may be in the best interest of the bank. Don't forget that the ultimate goal for the bank and the REO agent is the same—to get the property sold at a fair price as fast as possible.

What REO Agents Look For in an Investor

A big part of the bank's and REO agent's strategy of selling bank-foreclosed properties at fair prices as fast as possible includes dealing with reputable investors. Frankly, they want to avoid wasting time with the many would-be and inexperienced investors out there. Therefore, many REO agents often do little extras to keep reputable investors happy and buying from them.

So how do you prove yourself to be a reputable investor? Consider the following ways:

- Be straightforward and dependable
- Deal honestly
- Close each deal per the contract (unless a significant problem is found in the inspection and the seller is unwilling to reasonably compensate for it)

You also prove you're reputable by behaving consistently over time. This includes responding to calls from REO agents when they've found your kind of property: single-family homes in middle-income neighborhoods (with features as discussed in Chapter 6, "Finding Good Homes"). It includes consistently returning their calls in a timely fashion and making supported, fair offers on these properties. (This is where your cover letter comes in, as discussed in Chapter 8, "The Real Estate Purchase Contract.") Also, behave consistently during the negotiating process by following the guidelines set forth in this chapter.

The Reputable Investor Has an Inside Track

If you have established a solid relationship with the REO agent, then when your offer comes in second to an unproven investor, you often have the inside track. The REO agent will likely favor you, because you represent a good chance of getting to the closing table and buying the property with no hassles. This, in turn, results in two important benefits to the REO agent: (1) a commission for selling the property and (2) additional good standing in the eyes of the bank.

The last thing an REO agent wants to do is bring a bank a contract, get it accepted, then have the contract fall through or be subject to a lot of hassle prior to closing. The bank doesn't want to risk losing several weeks during the contract pending phase or losing potential buyers during this time and incurring additional holding costs.

Every REO agent is motivated to bring the seller a qualified and dependable buyer. Therefore, you must present yourself well consistently. Over time, the history of your transactions together should cement the agent's perception of you as a reputable investor.

REO Agents Provide Stability in Negotiations

We work with the same group of REO agents about 80 percent of the time, and we've learned how one another operate, so the negotiating game has become easier to play over the years. Even so, some REO agents represent multiple banks, so the game isn't always the same. A lot depends on the negotiating policies of the seller/bank involved. One bank may only make a decision after receiving three counteroffers. Another might be firm and state a bottom-line number up front, take it or leave it. A third might be one we've already worked with, so we can somewhat predict what will happen in the negotiations.

Certainly, the banks may change from home purchase to home purchase, but the handful of good REO agents who represent these banks in a community often remains the same, serving to provide some stability in your negotiations. So, even if the bank's selling philosophies may differ, the negotiating hints the REO agent gives may be helpful.

Get to know the key players, the REO agents, over time. Use their insights to help you negotiate well.

Building REO Agent Relationships

In the following example, we were negotiating to purchase a property through an REO agent. At this point, we had not established ourselves with this agent, so we were just another investor. We went back and forth for a few weeks but couldn't get the bank to agree to sell us the property. The REO agent then came to us and said that all competing investors would be asked to give a "best and final offer"; the highest offer would be accepted. We took this request seriously and made an offer close to our ceiling price (yet still below it, because the home needed a lot of repairs and improvements).

Then we waited for a green or red light from the REO agent. Instead, we got a yellow light. About a week later, the REO agent told us our offer was neck and neck with another investor's and that a slight movement upward in our offer would likely secure this property for us.

Initially, we thought we weren't being treated fairly, that this really wasn't a best and final offer situation. We weren't angry about the seller's sly move to encourage a higher offer; that's just business. Of greater concern, we knew this REO agent represented many banks and good properties. So because we had their attention now and our response could play an important role in how we'd be regarded in the future, we considered this request.

We had two concerns. First, we had not yet established a relationship with this REO agent, and we wanted our word to be taken seriously (i.e., a final offer should be a final offer). On the flip side, we wanted to establish ourselves as reasonable investors who were desirable to work with.

Because we still had some wiggle room before we hit our ceiling price, we decided to increase our final offer, and it was accepted.

This story doesn't end with the purchase of that home. After buying it, we told this REO agent we did this *only* to complete our first transaction together and start to build a long-term relationship. We made it clear we'd never again budge from a best and final offer.

This transaction began a long-term relationship with one of the leading REO agents in the local market. We have since purchased several properties from the agent without compromising our best and final offer policy.

OUR PHILOSOPHY

Be careful when assessing your ceiling price and initial offer price. For your first handful of properties, this assessment takes time and may even be gut-wrenching. But how you determine these benchmarks makes a big difference in the reputation you develop with REO agents and banks—which ultimately affects your profits.

Our philosophy is to be honest with and respect the seller and seller's agent (usually banks and their REO agents). If bank managers feel you're squeezing them unjustly, they'll be less receptive when you make your next offer. Remember that just a handful of REO agents dominate the bank-owned resale market in most communities, so it's vital to establish your reputation as an investor who is fair and easy to work with. When you do this, you'll benefit from repeat transactions from the same handful of REO agents. You'll establish yourself as a reputable investor who stands out from the average investor in their eyes.

On a number of occasions, our key REO agents and bank contacts have complimented us on the way we do business. Why? We believe it's because we follow the Golden Rule. We treat people the way we like to be treated ourselves—with integrity and respect. In turn, we believe our approach has made a big difference in our personal growth *and* in the success of our real estate business.

8

THE REAL ESTATE
PURCHASE CONTRACT

Now that you know how to make an offer and negotiate the purchase, what should the contract look like? What provisions are most important? Should you use a cover letter? This chapter shows you how to put your offer on paper.

UNDERSTANDING KEY PROVISIONS

An example of the basic real estate purchase contract we often use is provided later in this chapter. This contract has been developed for the particular purpose of purchasing residential investment property and specifically protects the buyer's interests.

When selling one of your properties to a strict purchaser (without our lease/purchase contract), we do not recommend using our basic real estate purchase contract because of its special provisions to protect the buyer. Instead, work with your local real estate association to source a contract that more equally protects the seller's and buyer's interests. (We discuss sales contracts in more detail in Chapter 15, "Selling Your Homes.")

Before you buy or sell any real estate with a real estate purchase contract, we recommend you understand your local real estate laws and each provision of the contract. A good place to learn is by talking to local real estate agents, attending real estate seminars for new agents and investors, and reading books on real estate contracts. It is beyond the scope of this book to walk through every detail of a real estate contract. Instead, we focus on pointing out some key provisions that differ from standard contracts that will likely be important in your negotiations.

If you're making your offers to banks or REO agents rather than to individuals, they'll likely need to transfer your offer onto their standard company offer sheet. This is not a problem; just be certain your key provisions are covered to your satisfaction and that you include the standard provisions of a real estate contract. You may want your real estate attorney to take a look at it for you.

The Main Section

In our experience, the main section is fairly standard. Section One details your offer price. Section Two sets forth your payment method. If you are planning to purchase the home with an investor loan, then under Section Two, be sure to include the terms you expect to get. For example: "This offer is contingent on purchaser obtaining a 10 percent down payment loan for 30 years at an interest rate not to exceed 8 percent." Then, if something happens to your financing source, you are no longer obligated to purchase this property.

Section Three details the earnest money you will tender when your offer is presented. The earnest money would be lost only if you attempt to back out of a deal simply due to change of heart and not because of issues with the property or your financing. We try to give as little money as possible, because it may not be quick or easy to get earnest money back in the event the contract is broken, even if there is good reason to break the contract. We typically give $1,000 unless the seller requires a higher earnest money payment. Even then, we try to keep it as low as possible. Sections Four, Five, Six, and Seven are standard buyer protection clauses (more on buyer protection clauses later).

Special Stipulations

Under the Special Stipulations section, paragraphs one, two, four, six, and seven are fairly standard; they are based on fairness and, in some states like Georgia, on tradition. Paragraph three sets the closing date (pick a date as soon as possible to impress the seller, yet give yourself enough time to get everything in order on your end) and spells out who pays the closing costs. Sometimes splitting closing costs or paying all the closing costs yourself is deemed fair, but you often want to ask the seller to pay and use this request as wiggle room in your offer. Paragraphs five and six are more buyer protection clauses. (We'll discuss these later in this chapter.)

The Final Section

The final section of the contract sets forth the amount of time the seller has to accept your offer; typically you'll allow the seller two or three days. But do not fret over the deadline, as banks that are sellers rarely take this seriously, often coming back with acceptance of your offer weeks after your deadline. It also includes name, address, and signature of purchaser and seller.

Although we allow the seller to acknowledge acceptance of our offer over the telephone, a signed copy of the contract is the only way to confirm the deal. Many lenders, mortgage companies, and banks require the loan to be in the buyer's personal name, not the corporate entity that's been set up. So check ahead of time with your lender so you are prepared to sign the contract in your personal name; otherwise, you may have to rely on the assigns language next to the purchaser's name.

Example Real Estate Purchase Contract

An example of a real estate purchase contract is shown in Figure 8.1.

BUYER PROTECTION CLAUSES

Buyer protection clauses protect you, the purchaser, from problems that you should not reasonably be expected to identify and account for at the time you make an offer.

FIGURE 8.1 *Example Real Estate Purchase Contract*

REAL ESTATE PURCHASE CONTRACT

1. PURCHASE AND SALE. The undersigned purchaser agrees to buy, and the undersigned seller agrees to sell all that tract of land, with such improvements as are located thereon, described as follows: The house known as 2846 First Purchase Drive, Roswell, GA 30076 according to the present system of numbering. Together with all lighting fixtures attached thereto, all electrical, mechanical, plumbing, air-conditioning, and any other systems or fixtures as are attached thereto; all television antennae and mail-boxes; and all plants, trees, and shrubbery now a part of the property. The full legal description of said property is the same as is recorded with the clerk of the superior court of the county in which the property is located and is made a part of this agreement by reference.

2. PURCHASE PRICE AND METHOD OF PAYMENT. The purchase price of the property shall be: one hundred thousand dollars. Purchase is contingent on purchaser obtaining an investor loan at 10 percent down payment with an interest rate not to exceed 8 percent on a 30-year loan.

3. EARNEST MONEY. Purchaser has paid to the undersigned seller, $1000 (check), receipt whereof is hereby acknowledged as earnest money, and is to be applied as part of payment of purchase price of said property at the time of closing. Purchaser and seller agree that the seller shall deposit earnest money in the seller's account by the third banking day following acceptance of this agreement by all parties; all parties have agreed that said escrow/trust account will be an interest-bearing account, with interest also applied to the purchase price at time of closing. The parties to this contract understand and acknowledge that disbursement of earnest monies held by escrow agent can occur only at closing; upon written agreement signed by all parties having an interest in the funds; upon court order; or upon failure of loan approval; or as otherwise set out herein. This contract is voidable at seller's option if the earnest money check is not paid when presented to the drawee bank.

4. WARRANTY OF TITLE. Seller warrants that he presently has title to said property, and at time of closing, he agrees to convey good and marketable title to said property to purchaser by general war-ranty deed subject only to (1) zoning ordinances affecting said property, (2) general utility easements of record serving said property, (3) subdivision restrictions of record, and (4) leases, other easements, other restrictions, and encumbrances specified in this contract.

5. TITLE EXAMINATION. The purchaser shall have a reasonable time after acceptance of this contract to examine the title and furnish seller with a written statement of objections affecting the marketability of said title. Seller shall have a reasonable time, after receipt of such objections to satisfy all valid objections and if seller fails to satisfy such valid objections within a reasonable time, then at the option of the purchaser, evidenced by written notice to seller, this contract shall be null and void. Marketable title as used herein shall mean title which a title insurance company licensed to do business in the state of Georgia will insure at its regular rates, subject only to standard exceptions unless other-wise specified herein.

6. DESCRIPTION OF PREMISES. Seller warrants that at time of closing the premises will be in the same condition as it is on the date that this contract is signed by the seller, normal wear and tear excepted. However, should the premises be destroyed or substantially damaged before time of closing, then at the election of the purchaser: (a) the contract may be canceled, (b) the purchaser may consum-mate the contract and receive such insurance as is paid on the claim of loss. This election is to be exer-cised within 10 days after the purchaser has been notified in writing by seller of the amount of the insurance proceeds, if any, seller will receive on the claim of loss. If purchaser has not been so notified within 45 days, subsequent to the occurrence of such damage or destruction, purchaser may, at its option, cancel the contract.

7. RESPONSIBILITY TO COOPERATE. Seller and purchaser agree that such documents as may be necessary to carry out the terms of this contract shall be produced, executed, and/or delivered by such parties at the time required to fulfill the terms and conditions of this agreement.

FIGURE 8.1 *Example Real Estate Purchase Contract, continued*

SPECIAL STIPULATIONS

1. REAL ESTATE TAXES. Real estate taxes on said property for the calendar year in which the sale is closed shall be prorated as of the date of closing.

2. GEORGIA TRANSFER TAX. Seller shall pay state of Georgia property transfer tax.

3. CLOSING DATE AND COSTS. Sale shall be closed on or before December 15, 2003, at such time, date, and location specified by seller. Seller shall pay all closing costs in connection with the sale of subject property to purchaser.

4. UTILITY BILL PRORATED. Seller and purchaser agree to prorate between themselves, as of the date of closing, any and all utility bills rendered subsequent to closing which include service for any period of time the property was owned by the seller or any prior owner.

5. WOOD-INFESTATION REPORT. At the time of closing seller shall provide purchaser with a wood-destroying infestation report, in the current form officially approved by Georgia structural pest control commission, from a properly licensed pest control company stating that the main dwelling has been inspected and found to be free of visible infestation and structural damage caused by termites and other wood-destroying organisms or that if such infestation or structural damage existed it has been corrected. The inspection referred to in such report shall have been made within 30 days prior to closing. The inspection and termite letter is to be provided by Nopest Exterminating.

6. SURVIVAL OF TERMS OF CONTRACT. Any condition or stipulation of the contract not fulfilled at the time of closing shall survive the closing, execution, and delivery of the warranty deed until such time as said conditions or stipulations are fulfilled. ** Closing attorney is directed to transfer this paragraph to the closing statement.

7. SEWER/SEPTIC TANK. Seller warrants that the main dwelling on the above described property is served by:

          * A PUBLIC SEWER _____ OR BY

          * A SEPTIC TANK _____

                   (PURCHASER) (SELLER)

8. WALK-THROUGH AND INSPECTION. Purchaser has the right to walk through the property and to have an inspection of the premises made by a qualified building inspector within 10 business days of acceptance of this contract. Expense of the inspection shall be paid by the purchaser. Should purchaser present to seller within this 10-day period a report citing any deficiencies in the property found during the walk-through or inspection, seller, at his option, may elect to correct said deficiencies, request purchaser to accept "as is," or allow purchaser to declare contract null and void. Seller shall have 48 hours to decide which repairs, if any, are to be made. Purchaser shall have 48 hours after notice from seller to accept seller's offer of repairs or declare contract null and void.

    This instrument shall be regarded as an offer by the purchaser or seller who first signs to the other and is open for acceptance by the other until 5:00 PM on the 18th day of November, 2003, by which time written acceptance of such offer must have been actually received by Andy Heller. Acceptance can be communicated this week to Andy Heller at:
    FAX: 404-674-9831
    PHONE: 404-674-9829

(continued)

FIGURE 8.1 *Example Real Estate Purchase Contract, continued*

> THE ABOVE PROPOSITION IS HEREBY ACCEPTED, _____ O'CLOCK ____M., THIS _____ DAY OF _____, 2003.
>
> _____
> PURCHASER SCOTT FRANK, HEIRS AND/OR ASSIGNS
>
> _____
> PURCHASER ADDRESS
>
> _____
> SELLER
>
> _____
> SELLER ADDRESS

Basic Clauses

In Sections Four and Five, you should not be expected to have done a title search to ensure that the seller has good title to the property. In Sections Six and Seven, it is reasonable for you to expect the seller to keep the property in the same condition leading up to closing as at the time of the offer and walk-through inspection, and it's reasonable to expect the seller to cooperate with you to close the purchase of the property.

Thorough Inspection Clause

Remember that our target homes are distressed properties. The previous owners may have abused the property or run out of money and couldn't properly care for the home. Therefore, ask for the opportunity to inspect the property thoroughly for any significant problems, including those that were not visible or simply missed during your assessment of the property prior to making the offer.

Under the Special Stipulations section, paragraphs five and eight protect you from unexpected, significant problems with the property that you didn't see or weren't aware of when you reviewed the property prior to your initial offer. We recommend you hire a qualified residential home inspector to inspect the property thoroughly for serious problems. These home inspections usually cost a few hundred dollars and can be completed in a few hours. Your real estate attorney should be able to refer you to a good inspector; otherwise, call your local real estate association or a real estate agent you trust. The inspector will provide you with a written report. If you find something seriously wrong, you can even present a copy of the applicable part of the inspector's written report to the seller when you submit a counteroffer.

You may eventually reach a point, as we have, where you have a high level of confidence in your contractors and feel comfortable enough to bypass an official inspection and the associated cost. However, we know we receive the same quality and detail of information from our own contractors, and the qualified building inspector language in the contract should be broad enough to cover them. Until and unless you achieve the same level of trust with your contractors, investing a few hundred dollars in a quality inspection is always a good idea and a sound investment, even in cases when the inspector finds nothing substantial.

In Georgia, we have big termite problems, so we also have a termite inspector take a good look at the house. Georgia customarily requires termite letters from the sellers at closing as proof of a termite-free home (see Special Stipulations, paragraph five). This provision protected us from buying one particular house that was about to cave in due to termite infestation.

You may be asking how we can have these inspection provisions in the contract if we're also offering to purchase the property "as is." The *as is* means that once you have thoroughly gone over the property with your inspector and have reached agreement with the seller on a fair price adjustment for any significant problems, then you will not hold the seller responsible for any additional problems you may have missed during your thorough inspection. After the thorough inspection, it's understood that the purchaser is then accepting the home "as is," because all problems are accounted for in the discounted sales price of the home to the purchaser.

It's Not about Nickel-and-Diming

Realize that the goal of the inspection(s) is not to nickel-and-dime the seller but to identify significant problems with the property that would substantially impact the value of the home and your profit margin. Unless we identify a significant problem that makes the property too costly, we avoid raising any issues after the contract is signed. That means we only go back to the seller with a deficiency report if the problem is *significant;* our offer price assumes we will find some small problems.

As noted earlier, our integrity and reputation are always being scrutinized by the banks and REO agents we deal with. There is significant value in being known as an "easy and reasonable investor to work with."

On the other hand, if we do find significant problems we missed earlier, we treat these surprises with the same professionalism we've displayed in other dealings with the sellers and agents. We simply detail them in our counteroffer to the seller, sometimes including a repair estimate from our contractor. Then, the seller must decide whether to accept our counteroffer, negotiate further, or tell us to take the deal as is or terminate the contract. If our point is valid and the seller offers a reasonable response, then there's usually no reason to be scared off by the additional repairs required. However, if the seller is unwilling to budge on the offer, then we usually walk away from this particular purchase. After all, we wouldn't ask for the price concession from the seller unless the problem was significant.

On several occasions, this step has ended the process only temporarily; the seller has come back and accepted our counteroffer after initially rejecting it. Sometimes, it's simply a matter of the seller waiting a couple of weeks to see if we are truly serious about walking away from the deal. Other times, the seller has relisted the property and had no takers, so the seller comes back and accepts our counteroffer. For distressed properties, time is usually on the side of the purchaser.

THE COVER LETTER

Now that you understand the real estate purchase contract, your goal is to make it as easy as possible for the seller to understand and accept it. The cover letter serves as a road map for your offer, so the seller can avoid getting lost in or confused by the verbiage of the offer to purchase contract (even though most of the language is standard). You also want to give the seller a basic understanding of the rationale behind your offer price. This is where the cover letter comes in.

In addition to benefiting the seller, the cover letter makes it easy for the real estate agent to read and assess your offer so as to present it better to the seller. Further, the cover letter provides a summary page to reference if you need to go back later and make a key change to your offer. Changes can happen a week, a month, or even many months later.

The cover letter expresses your interest in the property, then summarizes anything that's wrong with the property, listing the repairs and improvements you anticipate will be needed. The costs we use tend to fall on the high side of estimates, and we usually tack on another 10 to 25 percent for surprises—just to be on the safe side. For example, if you estimate repairs will cost $20,000, play it safe by assuming you'll end up closer to $25,000, and put the higher number in your cover letter.

If, after inspection and walk-through, you find a significant problem such as a bad roof, simply adjust your offer. On the cover letter, add a paragraph detailing what you found in the inspection and the reason for your adjustment.

The cover letter also serves another purpose. As mentioned earlier, we have purchased numerous homes months after our initial offer, after the seller tires of holding on to the property. The longer the property remains for sale, the greater the weight of the discounted price and the rationale for it. So, for a home that's not selling, we resend (via fax) our original contract offer and the initial cover letter once a month. When we do this, we simply cross out the initial offer date and write in the new date below it. After the seller receives the same fax several times (showing dates detailing their extended holding period), the odds that our offer will be accepted increase significantly.

A typical cover letter is shown in Figure 8.2.

OUR PHILOSOPHY

Our philosophy is to take legal contracts and letters very seriously. In this case, the role of the real estate purchase contract is to protect your purchase of the property, while the role of the cover letter is to provide a short explanation of your offer price in the contract. When used properly, the contract and the cover letter together should make a big difference in your ability to procure and protect your investment. They also should portray you as a reasonable, experienced investor, which should make an even bigger difference in your ability to build a successful real estate portfolio.

FIGURE 8.2 *Cover Letter*

Andy Heller
P.O. Box 1234
Atlanta, GA 30000
Tel: 770-547-3479
Fax: 770-548-9761

DATE : October 8, 2003
TO   : Rob Eichner—Schmid Properties (REO agent)
FROM: Andy Heller
RE   : 2846 Maurice Drive, Jonesboro, GA 32005
Number of pages including cover: 4

Rob, the following is my offer, summarized below, on 2846 Maurice Drive. This home has a lot of potential. However, I wish to emphasize a few key points.

First, this subdivision has shown a small drop in sales prices during the past year. It's not huge, probably about $10,000. Second, this house is a three-bedroom with an office, not a four-bedroom as advertised. The fourth room is simply not a functional bedroom (no closet).

The house will need approximately $20,000 in repairs/improvements. All flooring will need to be replaced, interior painting needs to be done, kitchen appliances are missing, a new master prefab shower is needed, the garage door will probably need replacement, some new siding is needed, and water damage is worse than originally thought. In addition, there is some concern the HVAC system may be on its last legs.

Terms:
- Offer $100,000
- Purchase "as is" (subject to thorough inspection within ten days of acceptance)
- Closing within 30 days
- Termite letter required. If not already done, please arrange to be provided by Nopest Termites, contact Suzanne Renner at 770-367-6434.

Warmest regards,

Andy Heller

9

FIXING UP YOUR HOMES

Which repairs and improvements should you make? What is the best way to get them done? In this chapter, we answer these questions and many more.

OUR APPROACH TO REPAIRS AND IMPROVEMENTS

Over the years, our ideas on what's right, when it comes to time and money spent on the property before we lease/purchase it, have evolved considerably. We make our decisions based on the following:

- Reasonable repairs that need to be done to get the property in good condition
- Improvements that are absolutely necessary to make the property comparable to others in the neighborhood

Choosing the Right Repairs and Improvements

As we've discussed, most of the homes we purchase are distressed properties that have gone through the foreclosure process. Therefore, most have been neglected, because the former homeowner did not have sufficient funds for upkeep or the homeowners simply took out their frustrations on the home. Consequently, repairs and improvements are a big consideration in our business, both in hassles and in costs, so we've had to be very systematic and sensible with our decisions.

When we repair the homes we purchase, we don't just do the bare minimum. We make sure the house is in good condition, repairing it to the point that our lease/purchasers won't have problems when they move in. We rely heavily on our inspectors and contractors to point out problems and identify items in the house that need repairs. Examples of run-of-the-mill repairs include fixing electrical problems, water leaks, faulty air-conditioning units, broken doors and windows, and so on.

We ensure that all the homes we lease/purchase have floor coverings (carpet, tiles, hardwoods) and wall coverings (paint and wallpaper) that are in good condition. We also stay neutral with the colors (such as beige carpet and white tile) and use good quality materials (not the most expensive, but certainly not the cheapest, paint, carpet, tiles, etc.).

When we choose improvements for the home, we do so along the lines of what is expected in a home in its neighborhood. For example, many homes we buy are older, without updated kitchens, so we often put in new countertops and sinks as well as new appliances (oven, stove, dishwasher) to match other homes in the neighborhood. We rarely put in a new refrigerator because people like to pick out refrigerators for themselves. Also, should the lease/purchaser break the lease/purchase agreement and leave on bad terms, the refrigerator can be removed easily, unlike other appliances that are usually fixed in place. Updating bathrooms usually proves to be a good investment. Additionally, if the backyard is partially fenced, we may choose to finish the fencing and fully enclose it.

Choosing the Best Contractors to Work With

When we choose whom to work with, we prefer small contractors who can do 75 percent or more of the work themselves. In addition, we have a set of specialists (painting, flooring, roofing, waterproofing, etc.) we use. By not hiring large contractors who hire subcontractors to do most of the work, we are able to keep our costs down and maintain more control.

We find our contractors and specialists through referrals from others in our real estate network, particularly from respected real estate agents and other investors. Before we use contractors, we talk to other customers to find out if they are easy to work with, if they do good work, if they complete their work on time, if their prices are reasonable, etc. We may even look at some work they've done. If we're comfortable with them after doing this research, we get a price quote and estimated completion time, then try them out on a small job. If their price quote is too high or estimated completion time is too long, then we might negotiate these items or choose another contractor or specialist. If their price quote is fair and the estimated time is within our target completion date, then we may have the beginning of a long-term relationship.

Once we've established a relationship with contractors, we send them to homes and ask for bids on all the repairs and improvements they're interested in and qualified to do. We request that they itemize each repair and improvement on the quotation. If the entire bid seems fair and we're comfortable they can do all the work properly, we authorize them to perform every task they bid on. If some items seem out of line or we don't feel comfortable that the contractor or specialist has expertise in a certain area, we often get another contractor or specialist to give us a competing bid. This way, we're sure to get the best bang for the dollars we're spending. If the estimated completion date is too long, we have others help out with some of the work. Our basic rule is this: always get the right people doing the repair or improvement. There is nothing more frustrating than throwing good money at bad work.

As a general policy, we send only one of our trusted and preferred contractors or specialists out to each home to bid on it. That person knows that a fair bid will get the work. We avoid playing games and getting into bidding wars with our proven contractors. Unless the contractor's or specialist's work slips in quality, prices noticeably go up, or jobs begin to exceed target completion dates, we see no reason to squeeze them on pricing and deadlines with each quote. We believe that everyone deserves a fair profit and reasonable deadlines in exchange for a quality job—especially our key vendors. By approaching our contractor

R *e a l - L i f e* E *x a m p l e*

We purchased a house needing waterproofing to prevent leaks in the basement when it rained. To get the waterproofing done, we obtained several bids and went with a company that had a solid reputation in town, even though it didn't give the lowest bid. This company stood out from the others because of its name and the fact that it provided a lifetime warranty that could be transferred to cover its work. We were able to turn that guaranty into a marketing tactic by assuring prospective buyers that any problems in the future would be covered at no cost to them. We know that, in the Atlanta market, waterproofing is a huge issue, and many buyers are scared of having to spend thousands of unplanned dollars to deal with leaks.

Additionally, for repairs that are hard to observe (like waterproofing), hiring a well-known contractor can be valuable, regardless of price. By going with the locally recognized leader in this field, we conveyed confidence to the prospective lease/purchasers that all of the work was first class.

relationships this way, they see we are fair and treat them with respect. In return, they tend to do the same for us. This leads to lasting, long-term relationships that are satisfying and profitable for everyone involved.

If you follow the guidelines in this chapter, then over time your repair/improvement process will become systemized. It gets much easier as your contractors and specialists better understand your business and what you want to accomplish. They'll even begin to give you more options to consider, and you'll establish a level of trust that allows them some leeway to suggest and pick out appropriate materials and colors. The result for you, the investor, will be a higher quality home that yields a maximum lease/purchase price.

Timing Paying Your Contractor

One of the earliest lessons we learned was to be very careful about when and how much you pay contractors, particularly in the early stages of establishing a relationship. With many contractual relationships today, full payment is made once the job has been completed. Home improve-

---

R *e a l - L i f e* **E** *x a m p l e*

THE RUNAWAY CONTRACTOR

On the first property we purchased together, we used a contractor who had done a little work for Scott in the past year. Scott was content with his work, and he had done nothing to prove himself unreliable. The repairs needed were extensive, so we gave him a fairly substantial sum to begin the work. The up-front money would cover the costs of carpeting, paint supplies, ceiling fans, and a stipend for labor. He did begin the work, but before long, he left town and went to Florida for six weeks. We had to employ another contractor to finish the job.

---

ment differs significantly. With larger jobs, it's rare to find a contractor who will not need up-front money (a down payment) to get started as well as periodic payments as the work progresses. As a general rule, do not give more than 25 to 40 percent of the estimate in up-front money—try to keep it to 25 to 30 percent for new contractors. Always reserve a minimum of 25 percent for job completion.

Be careful how much you give contractors up front. We also offer to purchase our own raw materials like flooring, cabinets, and HVAC systems, reducing the amount of money we needed to front our contractors. When a contractor's primary expense is labor rather than raw materials, it's much easier to spread out the payments as the contractor completes the work. This minimizes the up-front money required and any potential loss for you.

Timing the Repairs and Improvements

Once our lease/option offer has been accepted, we move at full speed because "Time is money." We systematically make sure we have all of our repair/improvement costs, plans, and contractors arranged as soon as possible. We often have the work contracted and scheduled prior to closing so that the work can begin immediately afterward. In fact, if we close in the morning, we try to get the contractors to start working on the property later that same day.

Offering an Improvement Allowance

For many of the homes we've sold in recent years, we've come up with a concept we call an improvement allowance. Rather than spending $5,000 on improvements, for example, we take care of the basics (to the tune of $2,000) and give the tenants an allowance of $3,000 toward future upgrades. We use this primarily for homes with a number of questionable needs or that have items that are passable but could use some upgrading. Examples include dated yet functional bathrooms, walls painted with decent colors that are not neutral, landscaping upgrades, etc.

Offering an improvement allowance has proven to be an excellent marketing tool. It's a way to empower lease/purchasers to get what they want right away when they move in instead of waiting until they can afford it. This allowance can play a key role in transforming a good home into a great home in the eyes of prospective lease/purchasers, especially because they can spend the allowance on something of highest value to them. It can also be a great tool to keep prospects from walking away over one issue with the home.

A key consideration when offering an improvement allowance is the need to protect the value of the home. Painting certain colors on the walls, installing certain types of carpet, knocking out specific walls, etc., may actually decrease the value of the home. This is why we reserve the right to approve all improvements *in writing* prior to work beginning on the lease/purchaser's chosen improvements.

R *e a l - L i f e* E *x a m p l e*

One prospective lease/purchaser was interested in lease/purchasing one of our homes, but the backyard needed to be fenced in for the dog. By listening carefully, we realized the dog held a very important place in this prospect's family. Here was a potential lease/purchaser with credit problems looking for a fresh start, yet a key concern was having a place for the family dog to run. So we agreed to pay up to $1,000 toward building a fence, and they would pay the rest. In the end, it was a win-win situation for everyone. They were able to lease/purchase a house with a fenced backyard, and we were able to get a good lease/purchaser—and add value to one of our homes at a decent price.

Approving Improvements by the Lease/Purchaser

As mentioned earlier, a lease/purchase is a gray area between renting and owning. The lease/purchasers are not quite renters, but they also don't yet have all the rights and privileges of ownership. However, we often allow them to make improvements to the property at our cost. In fact, we have had them ask to paint rooms, upgrade bathrooms, finish basements, cut down trees for play areas, and much more. We simply require them to write out their plans in advance so we can approve them. We want to make sure that, in the event that they do not purchase the home, their upgrades will actually add value to the property.

This approach creates another win-win situation. The lease/purchasers get to make the house more like home, and we get happy lease/purchasers, which usually leads to good things. In fact, we have found that those who invest in upgrades to the homes are more likely to purchase the homes and be better tenants along the way. As investors, in the event the lease/purchaser doesn't exercise the purchase option, we also get back an asset that's valued higher.

You'll find that not all improvements add value to the property. It's important to find out if the lease/purchaser plans any major improvement that might detract from the value of the property. This situation is rare, but you might need to ask tenants to wait until they exercise their

R e a l - L i f e   E x a m p l e

In one of our first homes, we repainted the entire house (inside and out) before lease/purchasing it. Within a month of moving in, the new lease/purchasers submitted a request to repaint the entire house (inside and out). Some of the colors they planned to use were not what we would have chosen. Fortunately, they asked for our permission. We agreed that, in the event they didn't purchase the home, they would pay the cost of restoring some of the interior walls to a neutral color.

We've learned to define these arrangements before approving lease/purchasers' proposed upgrades; there's always the chance they won't exercise their purchase option. In this case, the lease/purchasers did choose to buy the home, and the color of the walls became a nonissue.

purchase option before doing a particular improvement—one that, in your mind, would actually detract from the value of the property. Alternatively, look for a compromise solution.

IMPACT OF HOME IMPROVEMENTS ON THE NEIGHBORHOOD

Many of the homes we purchase are distressed properties and have become eyesores in their neighborhoods. The neighbors have watched the properties deteriorate and are concerned about the effect on their own property value. Because we often buy the ugliest home on the block and make it look good, we leave a positive impact on the whole neighborhood. If we had a quarter for every "thank-you" from a neighbor, we'd probably have a nice down payment for another house.

Additionally, when curious neighbors come by, our contractor is happy to engage in conversations with them about the planned repairs and improvements. He gives them a flyer we have placed in the home and answers any basic questions about the property and us, its owners. For detailed questions on lease/purchase terms, our contractors recommend that curious neighbors give us a call. Sometimes, they're more than just curious; they're asking because they have a friend interested in moving into the neighborhood. This approach builds a lot of goodwill for us. Our advice is to build a good reputation in the neighborhood. It's not only the right thing to do, it's also profitable.

PROTECTING THE HOME'S VALUE

After all of the repairs and improvements have been made, you want to maximize your chances that the lease/purchasers will take good care of your home in case they choose not to purchase it. One way is to visit the home from time to time (always giving the lease/purchasers notice) and to make friends with the neighbors who can keep an eye on it for you (at least the outside).

Another way is to get a security deposit, typically equal to one month's rent. The security deposit is refunded to the lease/purchasers when the house is returned to you in good condition. If they leave anything in the

FIGURE 9.1 *Home Inspection Checklist*

Home Inspection Checklist for		
1234 Carrie Drive, Decatur, GA 30987		
Room	**Problem Item**	**Specific Problem**
Kitchen	Vinyl	Small tear by door to garage
Living Room	Wall	Small discoloration by corner window
Bedroom #1	Carpet	Small stain in closet
Bedroom #2	Window	Small crack in glass (no air coming in)
Garage	Door	Small crack in second panel
Foyer	Hardwood floors	Small discoloration by door

_____	_____	_____	_____
Management	Date	Resident	Date

house that needs to be repaired, replaced, or repainted (beyond ordinary wear and tear), you apply the security deposit to these costs. To avoid an argument that certain items were already in poor condition, take some pictures of the home (inside and outside) prior to the new people moving in. Also, use a home inspection checklist (see Figure 9.1), which allows the lease/purchasers to document problems before moving in. The home inspection checklist can take many forms.

OUR PHILOSOPHY

A flexible approach to repairs and improvements evolved because we listened to what prospective and current lease/purchasers had to say. As with the fence example described earlier, we like to take any reasonable objection or concern and turn it into an opportunity. Although we know our basic formula works well, we're always tinkering with it. After all, finding the right people for our homes is like gold to us—we certainly don't want to lose them due to an objection or wish that we can resolve easily with a creative adjustment.

Ultimately, most lease/purchasers simply want a house that meets their needs. Therefore, making appropriate repairs and allowing for certain improvements can make a big difference for your lease/purchasers—and ultimately make an even bigger difference in your profits. Why?

Because you'll be able to attract and keep the people you want in the property.

Everyone wants to have pride in where they live. Any unkempt homes in a neighborhood stand out more than the nice homes and adversely affect the impression of the entire block. That's why this approach makes a difference for the neighbors and the neighborhood.

You can leave not only a positive visual effect but a financial one as well. By eliminating eyesores on the block, you help the entire neighborhood avoid unnecessary deterioration in property values. This, in turn, should also affect your profits because, using the example you set, neighbors are encouraged to maintain and improve their own homes, too.

10

OUR LEASE/PURCHASE PROGRAM

How do I maximize the value of the home I just purchased? Do I rent it? Do I sell it? We recommend that you do both, rent *and* sell it by using our special lease/purchase program. This chapter tells you why and how.

WHY LEASE/PURCHASE?

Renting and selling homes are both proven methods of making money in real estate. However, both have their drawbacks.

Investors who buy and then strictly rent their properties run the risk that they will bring in bad tenants who don't pay their rent and who trash the home. Further, purely leasing or renting is a slow way to grow your real estate business, because the cash inflows are much smaller than those you get when you sell properties.

On the other hand, investors who buy and strictly sell (known as flipping properties) run the risk that their homes may not sell for many, many months. That delay can eat into their profits due to holding costs (mortgage payments, utilities, etc.), which may lead to discounting the property just to get it sold. Additionally, the cash inflow is very irregular (not monthly like the investor who rents), and many, many months and even years can pass between cash inflows from property sales.

The lease/purchase combines much of the best of both renting and selling, and actually improves on them. It provides a vehicle to get a good, consistent cash inflow (monthly), get optimal tenants (who pay their rent on time and take care of your home), and eventually sell the home for fair market value (i.e., without discounting).

Our long-term goal for each property is to sell it at a fair price and profit, but our short-term goal is to get good people into the home quickly and get the cash flowing. If someone wants to buy the home immediately in response to one of our lease/purchase ads, we typically sell it to that buyer at fair market value (or close to it) and take the large profit and cash infusion. However, if the home doesn't sell quickly, we lease it and give the tenant the option to purchase, hence the lease/purchase.

The lease/purchase also allows owners to generate good profit (see the six profit sources below) and cash flow quickly. The reason lease/purchase homes tend to go much faster than homes for sale is that the amount of money and good credit to get into these homes is usually much less and far fewer good lease/purchase homes are on the market. Therefore, lease/purchasers are able and willing to move quickly to close on these deals. Your holding costs (utilities and mortgage payments) are minimized while the home sits on the market, and you can still eventually sell the home at the fair market value.

SIX PROFIT SOURCES

As briefly discussed in the Introduction, our specific formula for acquiring properties and our unique lease/purchase program allow you to generate good profits and quick cash flows (as well as diversified risk) because of the six profit sources. While many investors rely solely on the profit and cash flows from either renting or selling homes, we get our profits and cash flows from the following:

1. Acquiring the property at a discount (usually 10 to 20 percent) then selling the property at fair market value as set out in the lease/purchase agreement

2. Creating a positive cash flow from monthly rent payments that are often 25 to 50 percent greater than mortgage payments
3. Writing off tax, interest, repairs, and other charges on our annual tax return
4. Paying down the loan with the monthly rent payments
5. Getting appreciation value on our homes when the lease/purchaser chooses not to buy or requests an extension
6. Obtaining option money from the lease/purchasers for the exclusive right to purchase the property (usually 1 percent of the purchase price)

In our years of real estate investing, this method is the best we've been able to come up with for ensuring that the profits and cash flows from our real estate portfolio keep growing at a stable, consistent rate. It also allows us to grow our real estate portfolio faster and more consistently than many other investors, who are either (1) strictly flippers and must find the few properties that are discounted at least 25 percent so they can sell them for a profit or (2) strictly landlords and must wait years for their positive rent cash flows to accumulate before they can use their profits to buy more properties.

OUR LEASE/PURCHASE PROGRAM VERSUS OTHERS

Our goal is to provide reasonable lease and purchase terms to good people while still making a fair profit for ourselves.

Unfortunately, many of the lease/purchases offered by other investors prey on first-time, credit-challenged, and cash-poor buyers. We'll start with some examples of these so you can better appreciate our terms when we present them.

Other Programs

The following two examples show the games other investors play to take advantage of unsuspecting lease/purchasers.

The sales price is tied to a future appraisal. One type of lease/purchase term is "a sales price established by an independent appraiser at the time the option to purchase is exercised." The appraiser is chosen by the investor. For the unsophisticated buyer, an independent appraisal at a later date seems reasonable—but beware. Most who have obtained an appraisal know what an inexact science it really is. In fact, often the appraised value of a home turns out to be whatever the person hiring the appraiser wants it to be (within reason) or at least close to it. In this case, the person hiring is the investor, and the "reasonable value" can come in tens of thousands of dollars higher than the lease/purchaser ever anticipated.

Some people also get penalized for improving the home during their tenancy, because they didn't know to get in writing that the value of the improvements (carpet, paint, fence, etc.) would be exempted from the future appraisal.

Accordingly, these future appraisal lease/purchases tend to force the lease/purchaser to pay an unexpected and often unfair amount to purchase the home. If the lease/purchaser is unable or chooses not to exercise the option to purchase, the investor does a new lease/purchase with new, unsuspecting people.

Hefty down payment is required. Many lease/purchases require hefty, nonrefundable down payments (sometimes referred to as option money) of 5 to 10 percent (or more) of the home's fair market value (e.g., $10,000 on a $100,000 home). The target market for these investors is people with some savings but poor credit. The investor typically allows one year (sometimes two) in which to purchase the home. We've seen firsthand that this lease/purchase format may work for a handful of people, but that cleaning up one's credit to qualify for a loan often takes longer than one year (or even two years).

When the one-year option period comes to an end and the lease/purchaser is unable to qualify for a homeowner loan, the investor usually asks for another similar down payment in exchange for an extension of the option period. If the lease/purchaser is unable to come up with additional cash, the lease/purchase agreement expires and the tenants have to move out. The investor then goes about getting another hefty down payment from another unsuspecting lease/purchaser.

The bottom line on other lease/purchase programs. The above are just two examples of lease/purchase programs we've seen. We've heard of many others. The bottom line is that, like anything, there are many ways for an experienced investor to take advantage of an inexperienced home seeker, especially because buying a home is something most people do infrequently and the lease/purchase is something even fewer people are familiar with. However, we do our best to make our lease/purchase terms as fair as possible while still making a fair profit for ourselves.

Our Lease/Purchase Program

From the start, our goal has been to structure the lease/purchase program as a win-win for everyone involved. The following points outline the basic terms we've developed over time.

Fair market sales price is locked in. For our first lease/purchase, we had to make a number of tough decisions. However, the toughest had to do with the sales price. For this home, we chose to lock in the sales price at the current fair market value—no more and no less—and we have continued to do this ever since.

We lock in a sales price for several reasons. Lease/purchasers get certainty and fairness, because they don't have to worry about future appraisals. They also know a future appraisal won't negate their good care and any improvements they made to the home. Additionally, they have an opportunity to evaluate the value of the home before signing the lease/purchase. They can get comfortable with our fair market value assessment before becoming financially and emotionally committed to the home. We still make a fair profit because the home was purchased at a discount.

Psychologically, we've chosen to treat the home as the lease/purchasers' at the time we sign the lease/purchase agreement, because we can't sell the home to anyone else and they often do purchase it. Therefore, we don't allow ourselves to get caught up in the appreciation of other properties in the neighborhood unless the lease/purchasers choose not to exercise their option to purchase.

Yes, the lease/purchasers get the benefit of any appreciation in the property, but there's no guarantee it will appreciate. There's also the possibility (even if it is small) that the property will depreciate. In the rare instance that values in a neighborhood fall, you can be fair to the lease/purchasers by amending the sales price to the new fair market value. Because you purchased the home at a discount, you probably will still have some profit margin, and, of course, you also have the other four, undiscounted profit sources. Further, if the lease/purchaser has an option to purchase your home at a price that is now higher than fair market value, by not adjusting the sales price, you are removing some of the incentive for them to take good care of the home, make timely lease payments, and eventually purchase. We strongly recommend keeping your program a win-win, both in good times and in bad.

The option money is reasonable. Another big decision we had to make for our first lease/purchase home was the amount of option money. This payment is referred to as *option money* because, legally, it gives the lease/purchasers the "option to buy the property," while preventing the landlord from selling the home to anyone else during the term of the agreement.

In setting the amount for the option money, we decided to keep it reasonably low, so we charge approximately 1 percent of the sales price rounded to the nearest $500. For example, a $100,000 home would have an option money payment of $1,000, while a $160,000 home would have an option money payment of $1,500. Again, this compares to the $5,000 to $10,000 down payment that many other lease/purchasers require for a $100,000 home.

The lease/purchasers don't risk losing a substantial portion of their savings if they choose not to (or can't) purchase the property. For us, we expand the pool of good candidates for our property because we don't eliminate those without substantial cash on hand. Also, our experience shows that the lease/purchasers are more likely to take care of the home if they are not strapped for cash.

Rent is at fair market level. We charge the fair market rent for the neighborhood—no more and no less. Again, we determine this amount by getting comps on the neighborhood. (See Chapter 6, "Finding Good Homes," for more details on comps.) To research a fair rent, we call phone numbers seen on "For Rent" signs and in ads in the paper. We pull flyers and/or talk to local real estate agents, too. By providing a special opportunity for good people to own the home, it makes sense you should get good rent—the fair market rent—for your house.

We round our rent to the nearest $95 like they do in retail stores to attract purchasers. That way, a fair market rent of a $1,000 home would be adjusted to $995 and a $1,400 fair market rent would be adjusted to $1,395.

We've also found there are "000" ceilings on rents—meaning that it's important to keep rents under $1,000 and $2,000, even if the fair market value seems to be $1,005 or $2,005, respectively. While we offer our lease/purchasers a locked-in sales price at the fair market value when they sign the contract, we usually do include a 3 percent annual rent increase. We have found that rents increase somewhat each year in most places, and rent increases of 3 percent are so minimal as not to have a real financial impact on our lease/purchasers. On the other hand, to maintain a win-win situation and keep our lease/purchase incentives in place, if rents in the area stay flat (or go down), we can notify the lease/purchasers that their rent won't increase (or may even go down).

Applied rent goes to the down payment. We apply approximately 10 percent of the rent each month to the down payment on the home, rounded to the nearest $50. We call this the applied rent. For example, the applied rent on a house renting for $995 per month would be $100 and on a house renting for $1,695 would be $150 per month. For those who have trouble saving, the applied rent is invaluable, because it helps them save up all or a significant portion of their down payment. For all lease/purchasers, they feel good about having a portion of each month's rental payment go toward the purchase of their home. For us, even though we may lose a little money from the rent or sales price (depending on how one looks at it), we know we get people who tend to be more committed to the home, both in caring for it and in paying their rent on time (believe us, there is significant value in this).

If the lease/purchasers don't exercise their option to purchase the property, this applied rent is nonrefundable. In this situation, the lease/purchasers have simply turned into basic tenants who have paid a fair rent (not a premium) to stay in the home.

Security deposit is required. We usually require a security deposit equal to one month's rent from our lease/purchasers. However, if the people have extremely poor credit or we see additional risk, we require two or even three months' rent depending on the situation. The security deposit is an incentive for them to care for our home properly in case they decide to move out.

Our goal is to keep the security deposit as low as possible to expand the pool of good people for our property, yet high enough to motivate them to properly care for our home. From time to time, we need to use the security deposit for repairs if people don't leave the home in good condition. But gauging the amount to cover such items is nearly impossible, so we don't factor this calculation into the amount we require; we just figure it as a multiple of the rent.

Option period is approximately three years. Many of our lease/purchasers *plan* to purchase the home within the first year, but reality often diverges from their plans. Most of the people who buy our homes as a result of the lease/purchase option actually exercise it after two or three years, because they need the additional time to rebuild their credit and/or save up their down payment. Indeed, many of these people have consulted with mortgage brokers who have painted an unrealistically rosy picture to get their business.

The length of our lease/purchase agreements is usually three to three-and-a-half years. This span gives the lease/purchasers enough time to repair their credit or save enough for their down payment. We have tried shorter and longer terms, but we keep coming back to three to three-and-a-half years because people seem to prefer it. (Note: In Georgia, the longest term allowable for a lease is five years.) An additional bonus with a term this long is that we minimize the amount of time, money, and headaches associated with lease/purchasing a home every year or two.

Why do we say three to three-and-a-half years? Because if the lease/purchasers don't buy the house, it's best to lease/purchase the home during the best home shopping months (when the highest number of prospective buyers and renters are looking for homes). In many geographic areas, the best months are from April to August, because the weather is usually good and in the summer, kids are out of school. That's a preferred time for families with children to shop for a home and make a move. The exact time depends on the month we sign the lease/purchase agreement. A lease/purchase starting in October would have a three-

and-a-half-year term set to expire in April, while a lease/purchase starting in June would have a three-year term set to expire in May.

Fairness is the bottom line on our lease/purchase program. We believe that the terms discussed here achieve the goal of being fair to all
involved. You may choose to modify these terms from time to time and
property to property; just make sure to maintain the fairness priority.
Not only is it the right thing to do, but it also creates the right incentives
for your lease/purchasers to care for the home, pay their rent on time,
and ultimately purchase it.

SAME PROPERTY, DIFFERENT TERMS

Now that you understand the difference between the key terms of
our lease/purchase and others, the chart below illustrates the impact of
different lease/purchase terms on the same home. For our example, we
will assume a particular home has a fair market value of $100,000 and a
fair market rent of $1,000 a month.

Impact of Different Lease/Purchase Terms

Terms	Theirs	Ours
SALES PRICE	To be determined by an appraiser at time of sale	$99,900 locked in
OPTION MONEY	$10,000	$1,000
RENT	$1,250/month	$995/month
APPLIED RENT	$250/month	$100/month
SECURITY DEPOSIT	$0	$995
TERM	1 year	3 years

For "Theirs," the lease/purchaser is faced with an uncertain and
possibly unfair future sales price, while having to come up with a large
sum of money ($10,000) immediately. Paying a premium on rent ($250)
with the premium applied to the purchase (forfeited if they are unable
to buy) and only one year to clean up their credit (they probably have
credit problems; otherwise they'd have purchased a house with the large

sum of cash on hand). "Theirs" seems to put the lease/purchaser at an unfair disadvantage.

For "Ours," the lease/purchaser knows the sales price is fair and locked in prior to signing the lease/purchase (note the $100 under $100,000 for marketing purposes), only has to come up with $1,000 option money (1 percent down payment), pays the fair market rent (remember the $5 discount for marketing purposes), gives a $995 security deposit (fully refundable when they take good care of the home), gets $100/month of their rent applied to the purchase of the home ($3,600 after three years), and has three years to clean up their credit. Also, note that at the end of the three years, they will have access to more than $4,500 (applied rent of $3600 plus the refunded $995 security deposit). We believe that our terms sincerely give the lease/purchaser the best chance to purchase the home while giving you, the investor, a good cash flow and a fair profit on the property. A win-win for everyone!

Of course, there are many different ways to structure the terms of a lease/purchase, and the "Theirs" sample captures many of the worst terms. However, this example simply illustrates how "Ours" is fairer than many others, even if the lease/purchasers use only one of the unfavorable "Theirs" terms presented.

OUR PHILOSOPHY

We have consciously chosen to be responsible real estate investors. This means doing our best to strike a balance between making a reasonable profit off of our real estate investments and being fair to others.

Our lease/purchase program has enabled us to make a big difference in our financial success, because it allows us to reap the benefits of our six profit sources, including a good quick cash flow from our lessees and a fair sales price from our purchasers.

It also allows us to create the right incentives for people to care for the home, pay rent on time, and ultimately buy it. Of significance, we believe it has made an even bigger difference for the many people who are now homeowners or on their way to homeownership.

11

MARKETING YOUR HOMES

Now that you have purchased a home, completed repairs and improvements, and become comfortable with our lease/purchase program, how do you get the word out that it's ready to be lease/purchased? What do you say? Where do you say it? How do you get your message across? This chapter answers those questions and more.

THE LEASE/PURCHASE TERMS

Before you can market your property, you need the lease/purchase terms we describe in Chapter 10, "Our Lease/Purchase Program." We estimate our terms before purchasing the property. However, after we purchase the home, we continue to monitor the neighborhood for changes that could impact the terms. Houses may be selling like hotcakes, and we may need to adjust the sales price and other terms upward, or the exact opposite could also happen. Depending on the volume and types of calls we receive once we start marketing the home, we may also decide to tweak the terms to get the right lease/purchasers.

The following briefly summarizes how we choose the lease/purchase terms we presented in Chapter 10. We can often determine the sales price and even the rent by reviewing comps on the neighborhood. (See Chapter 6, "Finding Good Homes.") These price points set the stage for the rest of your financial terms. For marketing purposes, we always round the sales price down $100 (e.g., we would market a $100,000 home for $99,900). If you cannot find rent comps, a reasonable rule of thumb is to set the rent at approximately 1 percent of the sales price. For marketing purposes, we round the rent down by $5 (e.g., for a sales price of $100,000, the rent would be $1,000 minus $5 equals $995). Also, for both sales price and rents, we have found psychological ceilings on the "000" (e.g., $100,000 and $200,000 for sales prices and $1,000 and $2,000 for rents). Therefore, for marketing purposes, we do our best to price below these psychological ceilings even if we have information that shows we could get more money. For example, we would probably choose a sales price of $199,999 for a home valued at $204,000.

We usually allow lease/purchasers to apply 10 percent of the rent toward the down payment. So, if the rent is $995, then applied rent is $100; if the rent is $1695, then applied rent is $150. The length of the lease is usually three to three-and-a-half years, depending on the best time of the year to sell and rent homes (e.g., a March 1 start date would have an August 31 expiration date, and a July 1 start date would have an June 30 expiration date).

The security deposit is usually one month's rent (we might raise it during the application process if we like certain candidates but they have poor credit or rental history). The option money is typically one month's rent rounded down to the nearest $1,000 (e.g., if rent is $1,395, then option money is $1,000; if rent is $995, then option money is $500).

THREE MARKETING TOOLS

We primarily use three marketing tools to cast a wide net for the lease/purchasers we want to work with: advertisements, flyers, and signs. We sometimes use real estate agent databases.

Advertisements

When placing an ad, consider the following points.

Timing of the ad. As detailed in Chapter 12, "Finding the Right Lease/Purchasers," we tend to show our homes one day each week, usually Sunday. Most people looking for a home read the weekend newspapers, especially the real estate pullout section that comes in many Saturday or Sunday editions. Therefore, we don't want to miss the opportunity to place an ad two weekends in a row, commencing on Saturday (sometimes on Friday). We start the ad the weekend before our targeted first showing. This generates two weekends worth of calls. While we receive a good number of calls on Saturday and Sunday, many home seekers set aside the weekend pullout real estate section, then get around to perusing the ads and making calls during the week.

Remember, the goal is to receive as many good lease/purchase candidate messages as possible over the nine- to ten-day period (inclusive of the two weekends).

Placement of the ad. We place an ad in the "For Sale" section (after all, our ultimate goal is to sell the home), and sometimes we also place an ad in the "For Rent" section. Our experience shows that the majority of good lease/purchase candidates are scanning the For Sale ads in the real estate section of the paper rather than the For Rent ads. Also, most of the lease/purchase (and rent-to-own) ads tend to be in the For Sale section in our community. Get familiar with ads in your area by reviewing the real estate section.

Depending on how fast the home is moving, we sometimes place an ad in the "For Rent" section. The number and quality of calls received for the For Rent ad also provides some idea of the value of running a For Rent ad for other properties you market in the same community. If you are going to place ads in both sections, we suggest you use different voice-mail boxes for each ad to keep track of the type of caller so you can better tailor your response when you return the call. (See Chapter 12, "Finding the Right Lease/Purchasers.")

Content of the advertisement. The terms we offer make our ads stand out from others. We mention the basics (3 bed, 2 bath, 2 car garage, etc.), but mostly we emphasize the terms. By keeping our ads simple, we try to cast as wide a net as possible, so that we'll pique people's interests and be able to give them the full rundown over the phone.

Figure 11.1 shows an example of how an ad is worded:

FIGURE 11.1 *Lease/Purchase Ad*

ATLANTA By Owner
LEASE/PURCHASE
4 br, 2.5 ba, 2-car gar, big fenced backyard,
completely updated, incredible terms, applied rent
$119,900 $1,195/mo   404-123-4567

We prefer the phrase *lease/purchase* over *rent to own* because we've found the second term has a second-class connotation in some prospects' minds—it invokes rent-to-own items such as furniture and appliances. *Lease/purchase* sounds more prestigious, and it also doesn't push away people who look at the property as a straight purchase. However, in some communities or parts of town, *rent to own* may be the preferred terminology. Perhaps you've come across other commonly used terms where you intend to invest.

Remember, the objective is to have a good lease/purchaser in the home as quickly as possible. Therefore, if you think different terminology may be more successful in your community, give it a try and see what type of ad response you can generate. We believe in casting a wide net, so we consider each property and situation individually.

Note the "By Owner" designation in the ad. Some newspapers require it in ads run by nonagents. If not, we suggest you still use this designation for marketing purposes, because it implies that your terms will be better with no real estate commission involved. Of course, your terms *are* better—just for different reasons.

Also, newspapers usually charge by the line. Therefore, we prefer to limit the number of lines to four or five. With a little creativity, you should be able to get the key points into the ad.

Signs

As soon as we close on a property, we post a sign (see Figure 11.2) in front of the house that says, in clear, bold letters: LEASE/PURCHASE 404-123-4567. Sometimes, we include information on number of bedrooms, bathrooms, and so on. Like the ad, we try to keep the sign sim-

FIGURE 11.2 *Lease/Purchase Sign*

ple to pique people's interest enough so they'll call and give us a chance to explain our lease/purchase program.

Occasionally, we purchase a home in a neighborhood (subdivision) that requires posting a specific kind of sign. It may need to be a certain color, shape, size, or style. Sometimes, we find out ahead of time; other times, we learn about it when someone tells us on the phone that our current sign doesn't conform to the homeowners association guidelines. Either way, we do our best to find out what's needed and have our sign made to their specifications.

Flyers

As soon as repair work starts on a new property, we leave a stack of flyers with the contractor working there. Our contractor acts as an extension of our marketing program. Most know what we do and who we are, so when curious neighbors come by, they can answer questions and hand out flyers. It's common for us to get two or three calls from interested people because a neighbor told them about the home and gave them pertinent information from the flyer obtained from our contractor.

We don't use a flyer holder on our signs. Our strategy is to minimize the number of curious home seekers who write off the home without talking to us about the fabulous lease/purchase terms. After all, a flyer usually can't come close to generating the same level of excitement about our special lease/purchase terms that we can in a conversation. Additionally, a flyer can't answer questions that might keep the home seeker interested. We want them to call the phone number on the sign, talk to us about the home, ask questions, and make an appointment to see it. You also avoid constantly refilling the flyer holder.

When the home seekers come to our property, we greet them with a flyer as they walk in the door. At this point, the flyers serve a key role psychologically for the prospective lease/purchaser. These people are making many calls on homes, seeking both the right home and the best lease/purchase terms. If we've handled the phone call properly, by the time they come for their appointment, they feel genuinely *excited* about our lease/purchase terms and program. Yet it's one thing to hear about something—seeing is believing. The prospects are already excited about the financial terms of the lease/purchase and now come out and see our fine home (including the quality of work we have done or are doing). Our flyer then confirms everything *in writing* about our lease/purchase terms—written verification of everything we told them during our earlier phone conversation.

Figure 11.3 shows a sample flyer for a home.

Real Estate Agent Databases

Although we tend to avoid database marketing because it can be costly, we sometimes work with a real estate agent who lists the property in the local real estate agent database for us. We only do it if the agent charges a minimal fee (sometimes we agree to one month's rent), because we're only asking to put our property in the database, not show the home, advertise, or negotiate contracts on our behalf.

FIGURE 11.3 *Lease/Purchase Flyer*

1234 DIANA STREET
MARIE, GA 30319

LEASE/PURCHASE

- 4 bedrooms
- 2½ bathrooms
- 2-car garage
- fantastic location
- cul-de-sac living
- master with garden tub and separate shower
- completely updated
- large basement
- ask us about $5,000 improvement allowance

Schools: David Elementary
Danielle Middle School
Dennis High School

INCREDIBLE TERMS

$1,495/month. . . . $150 applied rent per month
$149,900 purchase with up to 3 years to close
$1,495 security deposit
$1,500 option money

Questions call Scott at 404-123-4567

In Georgia, the local real estate agent database is called MLS, short for Multiple Listing Service. Databases like this potentially expose your home to a lot of good prospects who do not use the newspapers to find their homes and may in fact be working exclusively through a real estate agent to lease/purchase a home. However, this approach may also open you up to pay a real estate agent commission to the lease/purchaser's agent, so be careful.

VOICE-MAIL MESSAGE

Because calls can come at all hours of the day, we suggest renting a voice-mail box. Be sure to select a voice-mail service without a limitation on the number of messages (though if you check regularly, a mailbox that holds 20 messages should be satisfactory). The highest volume of calls often occurs between Saturday and Wednesday, because the majority of calls come from your advertisements in the weekend newspaper.

If we have several properties on the market at the same time, we may use more than one voice-mail box to keep track of which calls belong to what homes. We also do this if we run two different ads for the same property (one in the "For Sale" section and one in the "For Rent" section), so we can tailor our return conversations to what the caller is seeking.

The outgoing message on our voice mail goes something like this:

Thank you for calling on our house for lease/purchase. Please kindly leave your name and the best phone number or numbers we can use to call you back. Please speak slowly and clearly when leaving your name and phone numbers. Have a good day.

Let's quickly analyze our outgoing message.

Thank you for calling on our house for lease/purchase. Please kindly leave your name and the best phone number or numbers we can use to call you back. This acknowledges the call and leaves simple instructions.

Please speak slowly and clearly when leaving your name and phone numbers. We began adding this sentence a number of years ago after we lost a lot of potential candidates because of heavy accents and slurred enunciation. Since we've added this sentence (and it's the last thing the caller hears), most callers are careful in their enunciation and many even repeat their phone numbers a second time. The net result is fewer lost calls due to incomprehensible phone numbers.

An important point: We don't give the listener any particulars on the home in the outgoing message. We leave this for the follow-up phone conversation. (See Chapter 12, "Finding the Right Lease/Purchasers.") We don't want the voice-mail message to be the only contact we have with the caller (in much the same way that we don't want the information on the flyer to cause an interested home seeker to walk away).

You'll find the best way to generate excitement about your home is through a conversation. That's when you can respond quickly to questions and comments. If you allow a voice-mail message (or flyer) to convey the information, it's too passive. Voice mail can't respond to questions and tones of voices. It may put prospects off and certainly won't raise much excitement. (See Chapter 12, "Finding the Right Lease/Purchasers," to know what to say when returning voice-mail messages.)

TIMING FOR HOMES NEEDING MAJOR REPAIRS

Just as timing is critical in determining a closing date on a property, it's even more critical during the marketing phase. Considering that mortgage costs on an investment property with a loan of $100,000 can be hundreds of dollars a week, adding an extra week between completion of repairs and people moving indirectly impacts an investor's profit.

To get the property lease/purchased as soon as possible after we own it, we place a classified ad in the newspaper the weekend before the day we plan to show the house (usually a Sunday). This timing allows us to generate interest a week or so before the first showing. We also usually put a sign in the yard and flyers in the house immediately after we purchase the home, even if repairs need to be done.

The fact that the ads cost hundreds of dollars each week (compared with signs and flyers, which are inexpensive and a one-time cost) affects the timing. It's critical to get the signs and flyers in place quickly, then place advertisements close to when home repairs are complete. This approach will give you the best bang for your marketing dollar.

If the house we buy is in pretty good condition and only needs a week's worth of work, we often start running the ad the weekend before we close. (Yes, that's right. To minimize wasted time, we begin advertising even before we legally own the property.) However, if the property needs major work, we wait until the repairs are almost complete before beginning our advertising, starting the ad the weekend before we plan to show the home. The repairs may be 75 percent complete instead of fully complete, but that's okay. We show a property as soon as enough repairs and improvements are done that prospective lease/purchasers can see the quality of work clearly and visualize the finished product. Waiting to place an ad and show the property once the work is 100 percent complete could postpone the move-in date unnecessarily. We also realize that the people we select may have to give 30 days or more notice to their present landlords.

The following example shows the importance that timing the marketing has on a property. We buy a home on February 1, and repairs and improvements are expected to be 75 percent complete by March 1. Signs and flyers are in place on February 2, and the ad starts running Friday, February 25 (remember to maximize call volume by placing the ad a week early). We return calls from the sign and flyers as they come in. We start returning calls from the ad on the second weekend the ad runs—Saturday, March 1—and show the home on Sunday, March 2. We take two applications during this showing and select one family. We reach final agreement March 5. These people give 30 days notice to their present landlord and set a move-in date of April 15. (Their current lease won't expire until April 30, but they agree to move in April 15 as a condition of us choosing them to lease/purchase the property.)

In this example, all of the repairs and improvements are completed March 20, and we begin producing revenue less than a month later or just over two months from the date of purchase (February 1 to April 15).

OUR PHILOSOPHY

Our philosophy is this: "When in doubt, don't undermarket." This means leverage all of your marketing tools: ads, signs, flyers, and even real estate agents' databases. Additionally, the timing of your marketing and the wording you use will make a difference in your results.

Don't shortcut or leave something out just to save a few dollars or a few minutes. Your goal is to cast as wide a net as possible to catch the right lease/purchasers. You will be amazed at how each marketing technique will make a difference in your success.

12

FINDING THE RIGHT LEASE/PURCHASERS

You have marketed your house well and now have people interested in it. How do you respond to the inquiries? How do you spot the right people for this lease/purchase arrangement? And how do you close the deal with them? This chapter gives you insights into doing all this and more.

WHAT THE RIGHT LEASE/PURCHASERS LOOK LIKE

Choosing the right people to lease/purchase your home can take a lot of time and thought. You are looking for good people—those who are honest, dependable, and easy to work with. Many candidates for your lease/purchase will have credit problems and/or little savings. However, the right people will be honest about their situation and able to explain to you how they plan on getting their finances in order. They will also likely have a good recent rental history and/or adequate cash coming in from their job(s) or other sources to cover their housing costs.

In selecting the right people, *do not discriminate* against anyone due to "race, color, religion, sex, handicap, family status, or national origin."

This is not only the law (for more information, refer to the Federal Fair Housing Act), but it's the right thing to do. If you approach this with an open mind, many different types of people will be the right lease/purchasers for you.

Of course, not being discriminatory doesn't mean that you can't be selective. However, it does mean you should choose people for the right reasons.

For our program, we are looking for people who want eventually to purchase a home, not simply rent. One big reason we don't seek renters is because they tend to think short-term and sometimes neglect caring for their homes. By contrast, renters with an option to buy are more likely to invest their own time and money to maintain the home properly— even upgrade it. We've found that lease/purchasers view themselves as homeowners even before exercising their option to purchase.

RESPONDING TO INQUIRIES

Marketing and advertising the home leads to many calls and inquiries over the phone. Here's our strategy for making the most of these inquiries.

Different Types of Callers

Your first step is to find out what type of caller you are talking to, then tailor your presentation to his or her needs.

Sometimes callers leave enough information in their messages so you know whether they are other investors, real estate agents, strict renters, strict purchasers, or—your preference—lease/purchase prospects. If they don't leave information that suggests their primary interest, try to find this out early in your follow-up phone conversation. You might start the conversation with this: "Hi, I'm Andy and I'm returning your call on our house for lease/purchase. Are you interested in lease/purchasing, renting, or buying?"

The following are the five main types of callers, listed from least preferred to most preferred.

Investors. If they say they're investors, they've probably attended some get-rich-quick seminar about acquiring properties at a big discount with minimal cash outlay. Because you're not selling at a discount and you're not in the lending business, you want to discourage this type of caller. Sometimes, they'll offer to take the home off your hands and lease/purchase it for you (in their name) with guaranteed profits for you. Beware. In addition to cutting into your profits, you don't want someone else to be responsible for placing a tenant in *your* home. If this investor has trouble with the tenant, the problem inevitably becomes *yours;* you'll have to deal with it indirectly through the investor you signed a contract with. This could get complicated, time-consuming, and costly. We have never considered subletting with an investor and probably never will.

Real estate agents. If the callers identify themselves as real estate agents, we ask them if they represent a specific buyer. If the answer is yes, we spend time explaining the deal we offer. However, most often they see the words *by owner* on our "For Sale" ad and call with a goal of securing our listing. We have never and probably will never hire one of these agents; we sell homes as well as any real estate agent we know, and working with them would take profits out of our pockets.

As discussed in Chapter 11, "Marketing Your Homes," even though the words *by owner* sometimes attract these nagging real estate agents, they're important because prospects know that they're dealing directly with owners, not agents. This works well from a marketing perspective, because no real estate agent commission is involved, making the home seem like a better deal. Also, some newspapers require their advertisers to spell out if they are owners self-marketing the property.

Strict renters. If the people say they're only interested in renting, then tell them about the features of the house, the rent amount, and security deposit. Look for an opportunity to convert them to lease/purchase candidates. Maybe they don't know what lease/purchasing is or how it works. Maybe they're under the impression you always need to have a big down payment or good credit now. (Read about other lease/purchase programs in Chapter 10, "Our Lease/Purchase Program.") However, if you can't convert them, then avoid spending a lot of time on the phone for the reasons described earlier. Remember, your goal is to lease/purchase or sell the home, not simply rent it.

Strict purchasers. If callers say they're only interested in purchasing a home, then focus on describing details about the house itself. Sometimes it's appropriate to say this: "We use a lease/purchase marketing format because it allows us to find good people quickly, but our ultimate goal is to sell. We do welcome calls from people who strictly want to purchase."

After learning about your lease/purchase program, they may ask questions about the terms. That's when you can convert them from strict purchase prospects into lease/purchase candidates. Also, convey that if they want to purchase the home, they need to act quickly; this home won't remain on the market long. They'll understand that you're not desperate to sell, because you can place good people in the home quickly with your lease/purchase program.

In cases when we've flipped properties by selling to strict purchasers during the marketing phase, telling the buyers about our lease/purchase program has helped complete the sale transactions quickly. It also enables us to achieve a fair market sales price (or close to it) because of the threat of losing the home to a lease/purchaser. When selling a property, be sure to use a traditional real estate purchase contract, because the contract you use to purchase as part of the lease/purchase program has some terms that may work against you. You can usually obtain one from a local real estate agent.

Lease/purchasers. Fortunately, the majority of callers will be interested in the lease/purchase program, so invest the most time with them. One of those callers could be living in your home soon. The rest of this chapter addresses how to respond to inquiries from this group.

Setting Up the Time to Show the Home

Choosing the right time to show your property can play a big role in finding the right lease/purchasers. As you'll learn, there's much more to the process than simply showing the home every time someone calls.

Choose day and time to show. We usually show the house only once a week. We do this for two reasons. First, our time is valuable, as yours is, so we manage it efficiently. Think of it this way: if the house is a 15-minute drive away and it takes you 30 minutes to show it, you could spend an hour to show it to each interested caller. You also have to factor in the inevitable no-shows—prospects who make appointments but fail to show up.

We usually schedule our showings on Sunday afternoons from 2:00 PM to 4:00 PM, when many home seekers go house hunting (after church, before supper, and at the same time as many open houses).

Schedule appointments. We schedule appointments rather than hold an open house. We've found that people are more likely to come and see the home when they are granted an appointment and know we're waiting specifically for them. We schedule the appointments back-to-back for every 15 to 30 minutes, often overlapping two or three appointments for each time slot. In our experience, one-third to one-half of the callers don't keep their appointments, so overlapping appointments isn't a problem. Additionally, we have found nothing wrong with having more than one prospect viewing the home at the same time. It actually helps us because it creates a sense of excitement. If more than one candidate views the home at the same time, we give an honest explanation such as, "We didn't expect everyone to show," or, "One family arrived early," or, "The other people have been looking over the home for quite some time."

Listening to Messages

We listen to the voice-mail messages generated by our ads almost every day (this only takes five to ten minutes a day, even when we have a lot of calls). For those calls that seem urgent (for example, someone from out of town calling from a hotel), we make sure we respond that same day. For others, we keep a list and return calls the day before we show the house.

We listen carefully to the message (sometimes listening to a particular message three or four times) to get the name and phone number correct. Just as important, we capture certain information on the type of caller (described earlier) and other information such as if they're interested in an outright purchase, if they're new to town, if they need a home right away, if they're focused only on homes with a basement, etc. We don't know exactly how we are going to use a lot of this information, but it can prove to be valuable (as discussed later in this chapter). Also, we keep in mind that we're looking for people who appreciate the terms of the lease/purchase and ones we can have a good relationship with. Believe it or not, this first message often sheds a lot of light on both.

Conducting the Initial Phone Conversation

In our experience, the first phone conversation (when the lease/purchase candidates are invited to the showing) is one of the most important steps of the process. We explain our lease/purchase terms and assure callers that what we offer is legitimate and worthwhile. We hope to get them excited about our terms and the home by the time our conversation is complete. This is why we rarely, if ever, leave lengthy return voice messages; we want to have an actual initial phone conversation. If we do leave a message, we simply say, "We've received your call about the lease/purchase and will call back later."

We believe the initial phone conversation is critical in building a successful relationship with potential lease/purchasers. Most real estate sales transactions involve a short-term relationship between buyer and seller, usually 30 to 60 days (from sales contract to closing). By comparison, our relationships frequently last three or more years. Therefore, trusting each other is even more important with this arrangement. So the first call should help convey that we're good, fair, organized, and dependable people. At the same time, we determine which prospects are interested and stable enough to be our next lease/purchasers.

Timing of return calls. Usually, we wait to begin returning calls until the day before we plan on showing the home. If we are going to show on Sunday afternoon, for example, then we'll start returning calls on Saturday starting at 9:00 or 10:00 AM and finishing late that afternoon or Sunday morning.

We wait to call until the day before the showing because we want our conversation to be fresh in their minds. We also want people to maintain the high level of excitement generated on the phone. If we can do this, then by viewing the home and getting even more comfortable with us and the terms, we have found that people are more likely to want the home. It's hard to maintain that level of excitement for more than

24 hours. If they're not excited, they might decide to skip the appointment or take a quick run through the house and leave.

Also, when we return our voice-mail calls more than 24 hours before the Sunday showing, many people drive to the home ahead of time. Some decide not to attend the showing at all because they saw an undesirable feature on the outside of the home—a problem with the yard, color of the house, etc. We're often able to overcome their objections by being there when they view it for the first time. Once their level of excitement wanes—especially when considering a big-ticket item like a home—it's hard to reignite it. Calling just 24 hours before the showing doesn't prevent these situations from happening, but our experience has shown it minimizes them.

Getting to know the caller. Remember, our first goal is to raise the level of excitement about the home and the lease/purchase terms. Key to this goal is *identifying the type of caller* (lease/purchaser, strict purchaser, renter, investor, real estate agent, or investor) as mentioned earlier. Our second goal is *getting to know the caller.* That's why we listen carefully to their comments and take copious notes. We refer back to those notes when we're selecting the people we want to live in our homes.

Introducing the program's terms. Many people have a list of questions they plan to fire at us during the initial phone call. However, the lease/purchase terms are the key selling points for the home, so we make sure we properly introduce them at the beginning of the conversation and stress their uniqueness. We respectfully ask callers to let us explain the program and tell them we'll gladly answer all of their questions once they understand what we do.

To set the stage and raise the level of excitement, the conversation can go something like this:

First, let me tell you what we do. We run a small company that purchases homes at a discount through the foreclosure process or other discounted means. Because we have already made a nice profit on the acquisition end and because we are fair people, we can offer such incredible terms. Our terms are much different than most of what is offered under other lease/purchase or rent-to-own programs.

This approach helps callers quickly appreciate the fairness of our terms and get to know us as straightforward, honest people. As we paint a picture of what we do, we emphasize the following aspects of our program.

- A sales price locked in for three years, as opposed to just one or two years or a price set upon appraisal at a later date
- No hefty down payment required, which shows we intend for them to ultimately purchase our home, not kick them out in two years and keep the down payment
- A fair rent comparable to others in the neighborhood
- A portion of the rent applied to the down payment

Presenting the home's features. Some might suggest first weeding out people who clearly won't be interested in the home (e.g., they want a flat lot, insist on having a basement, cannot live without a four-sided brick home, etc.). However, we've found that many of our lease/purchasers are willing to do without certain features once they hear about our fantastic lease/purchase terms. Nonetheless, we take this part of the conversation seriously and take time to thoroughly and candidly describe the home's features.

Asking and listening. In addition to describing the terms and the features, we ask questions and listen carefully while taking notes. We might note that prospect A is just getting out of bankruptcy, prospect B is just moving to town, prospect C has just started a new job, etc. This information proves to be valuable in the selection process.

In particular, we want to gauge their seriousness and appreciation for the uniqueness of our lease/purchase terms. We base our assessment on how excited they are about the terms, how many and the type of questions they ask, the tone of their voices, and their particular situations. We're looking for stable people, with good rental histories, who've been in the area for a while, etc. If they're interested in what we offer, they start selling us on the strengths of their situation.

By this point, we have gathered a lot of good information in our notes. Even more important, we have an initial gut feel for the sincerity, drive, and potential of the candidates. By listening carefully, asking good questions, and really thinking about what they're asking or saying, we often can draw insights into who they are as people.

Confirming appointments. We try to confirm all appointments the day of the showing (usually Sunday morning) and also confirm that they have our cell phone number in case they get lost. We use a cell phone number so they can reach a live voice rather than voice mail.

Checking messages up to the showing. On the day of the showing, we check voice-mail messages regularly, sometimes every half hour. Many prospects are armed with the local newspaper's weekend real estate section and may call shortly before they head out or while on the road. So we usually continue to check the voice mail from our cell phone on our way to (and sometimes during) the showing, just in case a last-minute caller wants to view the home. In fact, some of these last-minute callers have turned into great lease/purchasers.

SHOWING THE HOME

When we set up a Sunday afternoon showing, we schedule appointments back-to-back every 15 to 30 minutes (sometimes two or three at once). Again, one-third to one-half of the people with appointments don't show up, so our scheduling strategy allows us to manage our time efficiently by minimizing the gaps between showings. Of course, we always apologize to anyone kept waiting, explaining that, "We expected to have some no-shows." We then make every effort to give all the candidates as much time as they need. And we've found it doesn't hurt to have two or three candidates viewing the property at the same time. In fact, the extra activity tends to create excitement about the home.

On the day of the showing, we greet the people at the door and hand them a flyer detailing the lease/purchase terms. (See Chapter 10, "Our Lease/Purchase Program.") We show them around the house and take as much time as necessary to answer all of their questions, making sure they're comfortable with the terms of the lease/purchase and the house. This is a good time to get to know these visitors and allow them to get to know us.

THE APPLICATION PROCESS

Turning in a completed application and the application fee is the first true indication the candidates are interested in the home. In fact, it's often their first step to committing to the home. Here are some procedures that have helped in this process.

Completing the Application before Leaving the Showing

Our goal is to have every good candidate complete an application and give it to us before leaving the property. Just like any other type of sales, when prospective lease/purchasers fill out applications and pay the small application fee (usually $25), they are one step closer to committing to the property.

Some people immediately fill out an application and pay the application fee. However, other good candidates hesitate for a variety of reasons. Many are used to the slow-moving process that happens with traditional home purchases; others have a lot going on and are in a rush to view multiple homes that afternoon. However, if they don't make the small commitment to complete an application and give us the application fee that day, history tells us we've probably lost them for good. In fact, most good candidates who walk out of the house, promising to fax us an application later, don't do it. Therefore, we do everything reasonable (without being too high-pressure) to get them to complete it before they leave.

We stress that our terms are unique and that this home likely won't be available for long. It's common to have applications from other candidates already on hand. If we have a good one, then we might say we'll make a selection within the next few days (after checking credit and references), and they'll miss out if they don't act now. We assure them they can always call and withdraw their application; we'll simply rip up the check for their application fee.

We can't say how many times we've received a call a week or two later from an interested candidate who had procrastinated. By then, it's often too late because we've already accomplished our goal of getting good people into the home quickly. If we think a good candidate may be slipping away, we share one of our true stories about people who lost out because they waited. We realize there's a fine line between pressuring them and informing them—we just want to convey how disappointed some have been in the past.

Running Credit and Background Checks

The primary purpose of the application is to get information and permission to obtain a credit report and perform a background check (primarily rental history and employment). We take a moment to carefully review the application with the candidates before they leave the home to check for omissions or unreadable information.

Many companies specialize in running credit reports for their clients who've proven to be a legitimate company or investor. Their fees range from $10 to $100 for each report, so shopping around for the best price is important. These same companies often perform background checks. However, we recommend doing background checks yourself, so you can judge firsthand the accuracy and credibility of the information. In fact, many landlords and employers are hesitant to say anything negative in a reference. The only way to find out the truth about the candidate may be to ask follow-up questions (that often only you can come up with) and judge the tone of their voices when they answer them.

Unfortunately, some companies and apartment complexes won't talk to you at all; they do everything in writing. In these cases, be sure to find out what they need to share the information with you. Often it's just a copy of the signed application. Also, be sure to ask questions that will help you understand their situation.

Figures 12.1 through 12.3 show a sample lease application and verification forms with example questions.

FINAL STEPS IN THE SELECTION PROCESS

Choosing Good People

Obviously, we'd like to select the candidates with good credit. However, as discussed earlier, employed people with good credit usually choose to purchase a house outright—because they can. So the lease/purchase program often appeals to those with credit problems. When

FIGURE 12.1　*Example Lease Application*

RESIDENTIAL PROPERTY LEASE APPLICATION

This application will be processed and rated. Any omission or incorrect information may lead to a delay or refusal of leasing of property. Purposeful presentation of false or misleading information can result in removal from said premises by the landlord at anytime. Thank you.

Name (1st adult) _____ Social Security Number ___-__-____ Date of Birth __/__/__

Marital Status: Single Divorced Married　　Spouse's Name _____

Home Phone (_____) _____ - _____　　Work Phone (_____) _____ - _____

Name (2nd adult) _____ Social Security Number ___-__-____ Date of Birth __/__/__

Home Phone (_____) _____ - _____　　Work Phone (_____) _____ - _____

Name of anyone else who will be occupying this property

1) Name _____ Relationship _____ Age ____

2) Name _____ Relationship _____ Age ____

3) Name _____ Relationship _____ Age ____

Residence for last 3 years (list present residence first)

1) Street Address_____ Apt #____ City_____ State____

Name of apartments, leasing office, or property owner _____

Phone Number (___) ___ - _____ Dates lived there from: __/__/__ to: __/__/__ Rent per month $___

Reason for leaving _____

2) Street Address_____ Apt #____ City_____ State____

Name of apartments, leasing office, or property owner _____

Phone Number (___) ___ - _____ Dates lived there from: __/__/__ to: __/__/__ Rent per month $___

Reason for leaving _____

3) Street Address_____ Apt #____ City_____ State____

Name of apartments, leasing office, or property owner _____

Phone Number (___) ___ - _____ Dates lived there from: __/__/__ to: __/__/__ Rent per month $___

Reason for leaving _____

Employment for last 3 years (list present job first)

1) Name of Company_____ Address _____

Position held _____ Monthly income _____ Supervisor _____

Phone number _____ Dates employed from: __/__/__ to: __/__/__

2) Name of Company_____ Address _____

Position held _____ Monthly income _____ Supervisor _____

Phone number _____ Dates employed from: __/__/__ to: __/__/__

3) Name of Company_____ Address _____

Position held _____ Monthly income _____ Supervisor _____

Phone number _____ Dates employed from: __/__/__ to: __/__/__

FIGURE 12.1 *Example Lease Application, continued*

Credit References

1) Bank or Credit Card _____ Account Number_____ Monthly Payment _____
Balance _____ Phone Number_____ Contact Person _____

1) Bank or Credit Card _____ Account Number_____ Monthly Payment _____
Balance _____ Phone Number_____ Contact Person _____

Do you own any pets? _____ If so, how many? _____ If so, what types? _____
If not, do you plan on getting any, and if so, what types? _____

A nonrefundable charge of $25 is required for processing this application. Acceptance of application and application fee deposited herewith are not binding upon Landlord.

I/We certify that the information given herein is complete, true, and correct. This application must be signed before it can be processed. Any false information constitutes grounds for rejection of application. How soon would you like to move in? _____ _____ __/__/__
                                                        Signature of Applicant   Date

RENNER SERVICES, INC., IS HEREBY AUTHORIZED TO INVESTIGATE THIS APPLICATION AND OBTAIN A CREDIT REPORT FOR REVIEW BY LANDLORD.

FIGURE 12.2 *Example Employment Form*

DATE: October 30, 2003

TO: Human Resources, The Denny Company, Inc.
           Fax: 404-232-4545

FROM: Scott Frank, Ellen Properties LLC
           Phone: 770-303-4040
           Fax: 770-303-4041

RE: Employment Verification for Loren Weaver

Following is the signed lease application for the above-referenced employee. Please verify length of employment as well as present monthly salary. Any additional information would be appreciated. Please feel free to call me at 770-303-4040 to discuss or, if you respond in writing, to fax the information to me at 770-303-4041. Thank you for your time.

Sincerely,

Scott Frank

FIGURE 12.3 *Example Tenancy Verification Form*

DATE: October 30, 2003

TO: Leasing Manager, Barbara Apartments
            Fax: 404-232-4545
FROM: Andy Heller, CARRIE Properties LLC
            Phone: 770-303-4040
            Fax: 770-303-4041
RE: Tenancy Verification for Sarita Weaver

Please verify tenancy for the above-mentioned tenant. Following is a signed application from this prospective tenant. We are seeking verification of basic information:

Number of months as a tenant _____

Number of times tenant paid late _____

Please give details on late payments (how late, explanations) _____

_____

Is this tenant current with the rent? _____

Is this tenant required to provide notice before moving out? _____

If notice is required, how many days in advance? _____

Please feel free to call me at 770-303-4040 to discuss or, if you respond in writing, to fax the information to me at 770-303-4041. Thank you for your time.

Sincerely,

Andy Heller

we talk about credit problems, we pay special attention to judgments, bankruptcies, and large outstanding collections (from apartments, auto dealers, etc.) At the same time, if they don't have a Social Security number, then they don't have any credit and that, to us, is worse than bad credit. Having no credit means the candidates have nothing to lose if they walk out on their obligation or trash our home. We are unwilling to take on this risk.

Accordingly, after gathering information through credit and background checks, we often have tough decisions to make. Maybe one candidate has bad credit but commendable tenancy records. Maybe his or her job situation now compared with the past has greatly improved. We seek to understand the current stability, the excitement about this opportunity, the honesty in disclosing negative information, and other factors.

After bringing this information together, we follow our gut feelings in making a selection. In many cases, the choice is obvious. That said, we still keep our distance and avoid getting too emotionally tied to the candidate. We also make it clear from the beginning that this is a business relationship and we follow certain guidelines of good business.

In talking about gut feelings, we don't want to be misinterpreted. We do have a systematic way of finding good lease/purchasers—and we follow our instincts, too. Because we're involved with people whose credit has slipped, we realize they could be looking to deceive us—or they could be honest folks needing a break. How do we determine the difference?

The information gathered through our credit and background checking tells us a lot. Do they have steady employment? Do they have good tenant references? Have they acted with reliability in the past? Just as important, are they aware of their credit problems? Are they in the process of addressing them wisely?

Some people deny they have credit problems and may even be defensive about discussing them. By contrast, we're impressed with people who proactively tell us about their poor credit history (perhaps due to an illness, a divorce, or another life situation) and have a strategy in place for fixing it. Our credit application process also provides a good barometer; only about 50 percent of the people who complete the application include details about their problems ahead of time. Being forthcoming about problems with their personal situation is a wonderful sign. It tells us a lot about who they are and how they live their lives. It indicates they are honest, and we put a high emphasis on this.

Ultimately, we generally are looking for honest people who have acceptable rental histories and stable employment. These are the good people we want to have in our homes.

R e a l - L i f e E x a m p l e

A couple had just moved to Atlanta from California to lower their living costs. Tragedy had struck the family. The wife's mother had passed away, and her sister had died shortly after. This couple took in the sister's two children, making a total of five children to care for in their new city. Two of them were almost college age.

Within seven days of arriving in Atlanta, this family responded to one of our ads—on Christmas Eve, in fact. Andy spent some time getting to know them and learning their heartbreaking story. Although neither the husband nor the wife had a job in Atlanta yet, the background check showed they had worked hard in their previous jobs. Because the wife was a social worker, chances were good she could get a new job easily. They also had some money from the sale of their house in California, which gave us an opportunity to offer some creative terms for them to move in. However, the key was that they seemed to be good people. They had conviction, a sense of responsibility and drive, candor, a decent rental history, and a solid financial situation (money in the bank) at this point in time.

Nonetheless, because they were from out of town and without jobs, some additional security was needed, so we requested a security deposit equal to about three months' rent. This creative arrangement provided a buffer for us if their employment plans went awry (a win for us), and the family could move into a home right away and eventually buy it (a win for them). They have been great lease/purchasers ever since.

Asking for an Additional Security Deposit

We can't emphasize enough how important getting a gut feeling for people's integrity makes this business work. We are constantly honing our intuitive abilities and talking with each other about the other's impressions. So when we find good people, sometimes requiring an additional security deposit is all we need to get comfortable with their financial situation. Getting a security deposit equivalent to two or three months' rent may be what it takes.

Deciding Quickly

Does our selection process take a long time? No, usually just a few days. We can do the background check and obtain the credit report within 24 to 48 hours; then it's up to us to evaluate the information and use our gut feelings. With lots of practice, we've learned to get to this decision-making point quickly—and you can, too.

OUR PHILOSOPHY

From the moment we return the candidates' first voice-mail messages to the moment we select them to be our next lease/purchasers, we use every conversation with them to sell the terms of our lease/purchase and the features of the home. We also try our best to get to know them and for them to get to know us.

From beginning to end, we believe in following the Golden Rule— treat others the way we want to be treated. We act in an honest, straightforward, and dependable way, and we look for the same qualities in the people we select. We believe this approach has made a big difference in our ability to find and keep good lease/purchasers and to have good relationships with them while renting and afterward.

Certainly, we know we've made a big difference in people's lives by following our gut feelings and giving good people an opportunity to own a home at fair terms. Personally, choosing the right people (as opposed to the wrong people) for our homes has both reduced our stress levels and impacted our profits in a big way.

13

THE LEASE/PURCHASE CONTRACT

This chapter covers how to set up and use the *lease agreement* (often referred to as a Residential Rental Agreement) and the *option to purchase agreement,* which together we refer to as the *lease/ purchase contract.* They are kept separate to simplify the process and build in flexibility if circumstances change.

The sample lease/purchase contract has been developed and revised over many years and is tailored to the laws of Georgia. We hope you will be able to use most, if not all of it. As always, we recommend you confer with a real estate attorney before using the lease/purchase contract (even if you are investing in Georgia) to ensure that the contract fully and properly protects your rights in your state.

As part of our proven process, we request that all persons named on the lease/purchase contract meet with us to go over the terms before signing. In fact, to ensure there is no misunderstanding and to emphasize our sincerity, we carefully and clearly read aloud every provision of both agreements to them. Our goal is to handle all questions and issues face-to-face. We believe this approach minimizes miscommunication and has a positive impact on relationships with our lease/purchasers. We want them to feel comfortable about signing the contract.

THE LEASE AGREEMENT—KEY POINTS

The lease agreement we use is similar to most standard apartment or home rental agreements with one major exception: it extends beyond one year.

It's also separate from the option to purchase agreement to simplify the signing process. Most people are used to signing a rental agreement and are quick to get comfortable with it. Having a stand-alone document also simplifies the landlord/tenant relationship for a judge, should a dispute ever end up in court. Based on our experience and feedback we've received, we believe the terms are fairly standard, and they protect the landlord's legal interests (like most apartment leases).

The following is a brief explanation of the different sections.

Term. We set up the agreement to expire in the spring or early summer (prime home-searching months for most people) about three to three-and-a-half years from the start date of the agreement. This term usually gives enough time for lease/purchasers to repair their credit and save up the down payment. The agreement doesn't explicitly provide a provision for them to terminate with a penalty (such as two months' rent). We believe this is fair because we can't sell or lease the home to anyone else for the time period, so they should be willing to commit to us for the same period. (Lease/purchasing costs time and money.) However, to err on the side of fairness, we always allow lease/purchasers to break the lease with a 60-day written notice if they want to move out for any reason. We explain this to them when we sign the agreements. The 60-day notice makes it easier for us to get someone new into the home, because we're able to show the house while the vacating people still live in it. Homes always show better furnished, and demand appears higher when a home is lived in rather than vacant.

In addition, if we have not heard from our lease/purchasers before the last 60 days of the lease/purchase agreement, we call and find out their intentions. If they don't plan to exercise their option or don't want an extension, then we begin showing the home to prospective lease/purchasers while they still live there.

Possession. We put in this clause because if there's a delay beyond seven days (due to repair work, for example), the lease/purchaser is given reduced rent to compensate. Lease/purchasers like to have this contingency clearly covered in the agreement, further showing a desire on our part to be fair.

Occupancy. This specifies how many people will live in the home. We also have found that it's best to have only one family living in each of our homes. Experience shows this situation tends to be more stable.

Rent and discount rent. Rather than imposing a penalty for late payments, we offer a discount (usually $100) for payments made on or before the due date. We prefer a positive rather than negative approach to collecting rent . . . it works better. Our lease agreement is commonly referred to as a *discount lease*. The discount rent is actually the rent amount advertised, and the rent in this agreement is actually the discount rent plus the initial late fee (the $100). Psychologically, the tenant receives a discount for paying on time rather than a late fee when paying late. For the landlord, the net effect is the same, but the positive language works well with lease/purchasers. Additionally, in some states (such as Georgia), the courts will only allow the landlord to collect rent, not late fees or penalty fees. This provision allows landlords to effectively collect some late fees should a dispute be taken to court.

Late fees and returned check fees. It's common to ask for a late fee, and we typically ask for $5 a day after the fifth of the month. This is in addition to the initial late fee (the $100) if the lease/purchaser pays after the fifth day of the month (that is, after the discount period). We only accept cashier's checks or money orders. We usually make this a requirement because we often deal with people who have credit problems. Why do we include a $50 bad check provision in the lease? It protects us in the rare situation that one of our credit-challenged lease/purchasers still sends us a personal check, we decide to deposit it, and it bounces.

Security deposit. This provision encourages lease/purchasers to keep the home in good condition and ensures all utility bills for the property are paid in full. It also allows us to show the home during the last 60 days of the agreement—again, it's best to show a home with furniture in it. If all aspects of the security deposit provision are followed, a full refund will be made. Note: If you own a large number of properties (in Georgia, ten properties), some state laws require you to include the account number of your bank holding the security deposit in the lease agreement. This requirement varies from state to state.

Subletting. We don't allow the lease/purchaser to transfer this agreement to anyone without our prior written permission.

Utilities. The lease/purchaser is responsible for all gas, electric, water, etc., for the property.

Condition of property. The lease/purchaser acknowledges that the property is in satisfactory condition. This provision is used in conjunction with the Home Inspection Checklist. (See Chapter 9, "Fixing Up Your Homes.")

Insurance. As owners, we maintain insurance on the home. However, insuring its contents is the responsibility of the lease/purchasers. We always recommend they purchase renter's insurance to cover their possessions.

Maintenance. We expect lease/purchasers to take good care of the property, keep the same door locks, and regularly make sure the smoke detectors work. Because many people prefer to bring in their own refrigerators, we don't buy them for the home and don't guarantee they operate properly if we happen to provide them (usually only because they'd been left there when we purchased the property).

Eviction. If the lease/purchasers don't pay their rent, we can give them notice and then have the right to start the eviction process.

Abandonment. If they abandon the home, we are not liable for removing any personal items that may have been left behind or for rerenting the home.

Alterations. We retain the right to approve all alterations to the home prior to their being made.

Right of access. As in most leases, owners have the right to inspect the home during reasonable hours. We give at least 24 hours notice, but we do have the right to inspect without notice if foul play is suspected.

Attorney's fees. If we are forced to take the lease/purchasers to court and win, the lease/purchasers are responsible for legal fees. On the other hand, if it's found that we do not have good grounds for the lawsuit and lose, then we must pay the lease/purchasers' legal fees. This language is preferred by most courts when they consider reimbursement of such fees because it is viewed as fair (that is, loser pays). We recommend conferring with a real estate attorney before filing any lawsuits.

Limitation of liability and indemnification. As long as we are not negligent or performing unlawful acts, we should not be liable for injuries or damages to people or property in the home. An attorney can assess if this language provides you with ample protection under the particular real estate laws in your state.

Waiver and severability. This is simply legal language for helping us to enforce this contract. Again, an attorney can help assess whether this language works in your state.

Example Lease Agreement

An example of a lease agreement is shown in Figure 13.1.

FIGURE 13.1 *Example Lease Agreement*

RESIDENTIAL RENTAL AGREEMENT

This agreement (hereinafter referred to as the "Residential Rental Agreement") is made this April 14, 2004, between Marcy Properties, LLC (hereinafter referred to as "Management") and John and Jane Adams (hereinafter referred to as "Resident"). Management leases to Resident and Resident rents from Management, the residential property located at 1234 Danielle Place (hereinafter referred to as the "Property" and the "Premises"), under the following conditions:

1. TERM. The term of this Residential Rental Agreement shall be 36 months, beginning Noon, May 1, 2004, and ending Noon, April 30, 2007.

(continued)

FIGURE 13.1 *Example Lease Agreement, continued*

2. POSSESSION. If there is a delay in the possession of the Property to Resident by Management, Rent (as set forth in Section 4) shall be abated on a daily basis until possession is granted. If possession is not granted within seven (7) days after the beginning of the term, Resident may void the Residential Rental Agreement and have a full refund of any Rent or Security Deposit (as set forth in Section 7) already paid Management. However, Management shall not be liable for damages resulting from the delay of possession.

3. OCCUPANCY. It is specifically understood and agreed that the Resident represents that the family unit consists of two (2) adults and four (4) children, and that at no time will the Resident permit guests, visitors, or others to reside on the Premises for any extended period of time, and in no event in excess of fourteen (14) days without having obtained the prior written consent of Management.

4. RENT. Rent is payable monthly, in advance and in full, at a rate of One Thousand Ninety Five Dollars ($1,095) per month, during the term of this Residential agreement on the fifth (5th) day of each month (the "Rent Due Date") at Management's address as set forth below or at such other place as may be designated by Management from time to time. Rent shall increase at a rate of three percent (3%) every year beginning on May 1, 2005.

5. DISCOUNT RENT. If the Rent is received by Management before 5:00 PM of the first (1st) day of the month, the Rent will be discounted One Hundred Dollars ($100) to Nine Hundred Ninety-Five Dollars ($995) (the "Discount Rent"). The Discount Rent is to increase at a rate of three percent (3%) every year beginning on May 1, 2005.

6. LATE FEES AND RETURNED CHECK FEES. Time is of the essence. If the Rent is not paid by the fifth (5th) day of the month, Resident shall pay Management Five Dollars ($5) per day as late fee for each day that the Rent shall remain unpaid. Each daily failure to pay such additional late charge shall be a separate event of default. In the event any check given to Management by Resident is returned by the bank unpaid, Resident shall pay a returned check fee of Fifty Dollars ($50) for each check returned unpaid in addition to the aforementioned daily late fees, with all subsequent monies due and payable in certified funds.

7. SECURITY DEPOSIT. Resident shall pay Management a deposit of Nine Hundred Ninety-Five Dollars ($995) (the "Security Deposit") to be held by Management as a security for the faithful performance of the terms of this Residential Rental Agreement to be held in Account # 123456 in Great Hands Bank, where any interest accruing on the Security Deposit will become the property of Management. At the termination of this lease, the Security Deposit may be used by Management to pay for any damages to property (beyond ordinary wear and tear), and the expense of cleaning, if the property is vacated in an unclean condition. Resident shall not apply the Security Deposit in payment of any month's rent, including the last month's rent, unless Resident has obtained prior written consent from Management. Nothing in this Residential Rental Agreement shall preclude Management from retaining the Security Deposit for nonpayment of rent or of fees, for the abandonment of the Premises, for nonpayment of utility charges, for repair work or cleaning contracted by Resident with a third party, or for actual damages caused by Resident's breaching this Residential Rental Agreement. The balance, if any, of the Security Deposit shall be refunded to Resident within thirty (30) days after termination of this Residential Rental Agreement provided that: (A) no damages exist above normal wear and tear; (B) the Premises, including all carpets, walls, floors, appliances, and bathroom fixtures, have been thoroughly cleaned; (C) Resident allows Management to show Premises during the last sixty (60) days of this Residential Rental Agreement, provided that Management gives Resident at least 24 hours prior notice; (D) all monies due Management by Resident have been paid to Management; and (E) Resident has paid all final bills, including all utility bills, that have been Resident's responsibility during this Residential Rental Agreement.

FIGURE 13.1 *Example Lease Agreement, continued*

8. SUBLETTING. Resident agrees that it will not assign, sublet, or transfer the Property or any part thereof without the Management's prior written consent.

9. UTILITIES. Resident shall be responsible and pay for all utilities and other services supplied to the Property. 10. CONDITION OF PROPERTY. Resident agrees that the Property is in a condition satisfactory for the purposes herein contemplated and that the same is accepted without warranty or representation as to condition on the part of Management.

11. INSURANCE. Management and/or the owner of the Property (the "Owner") has an insurance policy on the structure of the Property only. Resident is responsible for insurance on the contents of the Property and is encouraged to obtain renter's insurance to cover such contents prior to taking occupancy of the Property. In the case of damage to the Property, Resident is to notify Management immediately. If the Property is totally destroyed or so substantially damaged as to be untenantable by storm, fire, earthquake, flooding, or other casualty, this Residential Rental Agreement shall terminate as of the date of such destruction or damage, and rental shall be accounted for as of that date between Management and Resident. If the Property should be damaged, but not be rendered untenantable: (A) to the extent that Management decides to make the requisite repairs, then Resident shall continue to pay Rent as normal under this Residential Rental Agreement; or (B) to the extent that Management decides not to make the requisite repairs, then the term of this Residential Rental Agreement shall end and the Rent shall be prorated up to the time of the damage.

12. MAINTENANCE. The maintenance of the property shall be done by the Resident to keep the property in good condition. The Resident shall be careful to ensure that the plumbing pipes do not freeze or are not clogged. Resident is prohibited from adding locks to, changing, or in any way altering locks installed on the doors on the Premises without the prior written consent of Management, and Resident shall provide Management copies of keys to the added, changed, or altered locks if Management does provide such consent. Resident acknowledges the presence of a working smoke detector on each level of the Premises and acknowledges that it understands how to test and operate the detector(s), and Resident agrees to test the detector(s) weekly for proper operation and replace batteries when necessary. Resident further agrees to notify Management immediately in writing if any detector fails to operate properly during any test. The refrigerator and window air conditioner, if any, delivered with the Premises are for the convenience of the Resident, but are not guaranteed to operate properly for the duration of the Residential Rental Agreement, and Resident agrees to be responsible for any repairs related to the operation of any such appliance. In the event Resident fails to maintain the lawns or shrubbery of the Property properly, Management, after attempting to notify Resident, may, but is not required to, maintain such lawns and/or shrubbery as Management deems proper, with all costs of such maintenance by Management to be paid by Resident.

13. EVICTION. If the Rent called for in Section 4 herein has not been paid by the Rent Due Date or Resident has failed to perform any term of this Residential Rental Agreement hereof, then Management shall, within two (2) days after providing notice to Resident thereof which has not been cured, automatically and immediately have the right to take out a Dispossessory Warrant and have Resident, his family, and possessions, evicted from the Premises. Whenever under the terms hereof Management is entitled to possession of Premises, Resident will at once surrender same to Management in good condition as at present, ordinary wear and tear excepted, and Resident will remove all of Resident's effects therefrom; and Management may forthwith reenter Premises and remove all persons and effects therefrom using such force as may be necessary without being guilty of forcible entry or detainer, trespass, or other tort.

(continued)

FIGURE 13.1 *Example Lease Agreement, continued*

14. ABANDONMENT. If Resident removes or attempts to remove property from the Premises other than in the usual course of continuing occupancy, without having first paid Management all monies due, the Premises may be considered abandoned, and Management shall have the right, without notice, to store or dispose of any property left on the Premises by Resident. Management shall also have the right to store or dispose of any of the Resident's property remaining on the Premises after the termination of this Residential Rental Agreement. The title of any such property shall automatically vest in the Owner. Management may, at his option, declare this Residential Rental Agreement forfeited and rerent the Premises without any liability to Resident whatsoever.

15. ALTERATIONS. Resident shall not make, or allow to be made, any alterations, installations, or redecorations of any kind to the Property without prior written consent of Management; provided, however, that notwithstanding such consent, all alterations including items affixed to the Property shall become a permanent part of the Property and the property of the Owner upon the termination of the Residential Rental Agreement.

16. RIGHT OF ACCESS. Management has the right to access the Property during reasonable hours without notice to Resident for maintenance of the Property and for inspection to determine that the Property is being used for the purpose herein described and to determine the condition of the Property. In case of emergency, Management may enter the Property at any time.

17. ATTORNEY'S FEES. In any legal action to enforce any term under this Residential Rental Agreement, the prevailing party shall be entitled to all costs incurred in connection with such action, including reasonable attorney's fees and court costs.

18. LIMITATION ON LIABILITY AND INDEMNIFICATION. Management and Owner shall not be liable for any damage or injury to Resident, or any other person, or to any property occurring on the Property or in common areas thereof, unless such damage is the proximate result of the negligence or unlawful act of Management and Owner. Resident hereby indemnifies, releases, and holds harmless Management, Owner, and their agents from and against any and all suits, actions, claims, judgments, and expenses arising out of or relating to any damage or injury occurring on the Property or in connection with this Residential Rental Agreement, except for those acts described above.

19. WAIVER AND SEVERABILITY. No failure of Management to enforce any term of this Residential Rental Agreement shall be deemed a waiver, nor shall any acceptance of a partial payment of rent (or any payment marked "payment in full" or a similar designation) be deemed a waiver of Management's right to the full amount thereof. In the event that any part of this Residential Rental Agreement is deemed to be unenforceable by a court of law, the remaining parts of this Residential Rental Agreement shall remain in full force and effect as though the unenforceable part or parts were not written into this Residential Rental Agreement.

In witness whereof, the parties hereto have caused this Residential Rental Agreement to be signed in person or by a person duly authorized, on the day and year above. No modifications may be made to this Residential Rental Agreement unless all parties agree in writing.

"MANAGEMENT"   **"RESIDENT"**

_____   _____

Marcy Properties, LLC   **Dennis David/Diana David**
1234 Brian Street
Ellen, GA 30111

OPTION TO PURCHASE AGREEMENT— KEY POINTS

The option to purchase agreement, unlike the lease agreement, is usually something new and unfamiliar to the family. Therefore, the goal with this agreement is to simplify and clearly spell out the terms. Additionally, because the lease/purchasers are no longer pure tenants and now have "exclusive rights" to eventually purchase the property, many homeowner obligations are transferred to them.

We have tinkered with the terms over time and believe they are fair. Here's a brief explanation of the different sections.

Expiration. This date corresponds to the expiration date on the lease agreement. Again, we usually give the lease/purchaser three to three-and-a-half years to buy the home.

Financial terms.

- The purchase price clause locks in the sales price for the length of the agreement.
- The money for consideration (or option money) corresponds to the value of the property (usually approximately 1 percent of the purchase price). Usually, we allow the lease/purchasers to apply this option money to the down payment for the home, but it is nonrefundable if they do not buy the home. We believe that it's fair for the owners to keep this money, because this is a small price to prevent us from selling the house to anyone else during the term of the agreement.
- The applied rent (usually approximately 1 percent of the rent) allows lease/purchasers to save toward the down payment by paying their monthly rent. This applied rent is nonrefundable if they choose not to purchase the home. We believe that letting the owners keep this money is fair because, if they don't buy, then they were actually tenants while they lived in the home. Therefore, the applied rent is simply a portion of the fair market rent they were paying (not a premium) while tenants.
- The payment schedule spells out how all monies will be paid. The flexibility that the payment schedule affords is a wonderful mar-

keting tool and differentiates our approach from many others that require all money up front. Additionally, as noted earlier, we sometimes require lease/purchasers to come up with an additional security deposit (one or two months' rent) to offset their poor credit history. Because we have advertised a one month's security deposit, we often allow the lease/purchaser to spread out the additional month(s) security deposit from two to six months. We specify the exact timing for these additional payments in the payment schedule. When setting up payment terms, it's best to apply the money first toward the option money, next toward the rent, and lastly to the security deposit. If we ever end up in court because the lease/purchaser can't make all the payments, sometimes the courts will allow owners to keep the option money and rent before they allow keeping the security deposit. Keeping this money is fair because we must now spend time and money to lease/purchase the property again.

Notice. We require a 15-day notice if lease/purchasers want to purchase the house, so we have adequate time to plan to attend the closing.

Assignment. The option to purchase is not assignable by the lease/purchaser because we want to maintain control over who lives in our homes. However, we can assign the lease/purchase to anyone willing (and able) to maintain the agreement.

Conveyance. Owners convey clear title to the property with a warranty deed that may include easements, such as the electric company's rights to run a power line over the back of the yard.

Condition of property. This confirms that the property is in good condition, to be used with the home inspection checklist. (See Chapter 9, "Fixing Up Your Homes.")

Repairs, improvements, and association fees. This is where many homeowner responsibilities are transferred to lease/purchasers. They must keep the home in good condition.

Eviction. If lease/purchasers don't pay their rent, we reserve the right to have them removed from the property and terminate this agreement.

Attorney's fees and closing costs. Again, the loser pays if the dispute ends up in court over this agreement. Also, the costs associated with purchasing a home are paid by the lease/purchasers when they buy the home.

Waiver. Owners do not waive their rights to legal recourse simply because they tried to work things out with the lease/purchaser before going to court.

Example Option to Purchase Agreement

An example of an option to purchase agreement is shown in Figure 13.2.

OUR PHILOSOPHY

Just like the real estate purchase contract, the lease/purchase contract makes a big difference in protecting your legal interests in your home. It should make an even bigger difference in putting lease/purchasers at ease with your lease/purchase program. They should now completely understand it and have everything in writing.

Because the transactions are legal in nature, we suggest you have a local real estate attorney review and modify the lease/purchase contract to ensure it conforms to the laws of your state. Also, make sure you fully understand it and get comfortable with it. When you sign it with your lease/purchasers, take the time to carefully go over it with them. Trust our advice on this point; it makes a big difference in the appreciation of your program and in the development of a good relationship.

FIGURE 13.2 *Example Option to Purchase Agreement*

OPTION TO PURCHASE AGREEMENT

This agreement (hereinafter referred to as the "Option to Purchase Agreement") is made by Marie Properties, LLC (hereinafter referred to as "Owner") in consideration of, among others, the faithful compliance by David and Danielle Scott (hereinafter referred to as "Resident") in connection with the terms of the attached Residential Rental Agreement and, specifically, the proper maintenance of the residential property located at 5678 Melvin Way (hereinafter referred to as the "Property"). The full legal description of the Property is the same as is recorded with the Clerk of the Superior Court of Dekalb County, Atlanta, Georgia, and is made a part of this Option to Purchase Agreement by reference.

1. EXPIRATION. Resident has the option to purchase the Property on or before April 30, 2007. This Option to Purchase Agreement shall automatically expire and be considered void after this date.

2. FINANCIAL TERMS. The financial terms of this Option to Purchase Agreement shall be:

   a. *Purchase Price.* If Resident exercises its option to purchase the Property, Owner agrees to sell the Property to Resident for the purchase price of Ninety-Nine Thousand Nine Hundred Dollars ($99,900).

   b. *Money for Consideration.* (Option Money) Resident shall pay Owner One Thousand Dollars ($1,000) as money for consideration for the option to purchase the Property under this Option to Purchase Agreement. This Money for Consideration may be applied towards the Purchase of the Property. However, in the instance that resident chooses not to exercise this Option to Purchase Agreement, then the Money for Consideration shall automatically and immediately vest with Owner in total.

   c. *Applied Rent.* From each month's Rent under the Residential Rental Agreement, Owner agrees to apply One Hundred Dollars ($100) toward Resident's purchase of the Property. However, the Applied Rent shall be nonrefundable to Resident and shall automatically and immediately vest with Owner, in total, in the instance that Resident chooses not to exercise this Option to Purchase Agreement.

   d. *Payment Schedule.* At signing of the Option to Purchase and Residential Rental Agreement, Resident shall pay Owner: $1,495 toward Option Money ($1,000) and partial May Rent ($495 of $995). Remaining $1,495 is due no later than May 1, 2004, toward the rest of May Rent ($500 of $995) and Security Deposit ($995), at which time keys will be given to Resident.

3. NOTICE. Resident must notify Owner in writing of its intent to exercise this Option to Purchase Agreement no later than fifteen (15) days before exercising the option to purchase under this Option to Purchase Agreement.

4. ASSIGNMENT. This Option to Purchase Agreement is not transferable or assignable to any third party by Resident, and can only be exercised by the Resident signing this Option to Purchase Agreement.

5. CONVEYANCE. Upon Resident exercising its option to purchase under this Option to Purchase Agreement, the Property shall be conveyed by Owner to Resident via a warranty deed subject to all easements and other restrictions of record.

6. CONDITION OF PROPERTY. Resident agrees that the Property is in condition satisfactory for the purposes herein contemplated and that the same is accepted without warranty or representation as to condition on the part of Owner.

FIGURE 13.2 *Example Option to Purchase Agreement, continued*

7. REPAIRS, IMPROVEMENTS, AND ASSOCIATION FEES. During the term of this Option to Purchase Agreement and the Residential Rental Agreement, as further consideration, Resident agrees to be responsible and pay for all repairs and improvements and to refrain from any acts or lack of actions which might result in any jeopardy or loss of value to the Property. This includes painting, maintenance of mechanical, electrical, plumbing, heating, and cooling systems, lawn, shrubbery, interior and exterior walls, doors, roof, and anything else necessary to prevent the Property from deteriorating in any manner and to keep the Property in good condition. However, Resident agrees not to make any major repairs and improvements without obtaining the prior written consent of Owner. Resident also agrees to be responsible and pay for all homeowners association fees, including swimming and tennis fees. Resident is also responsible for all pest control.

8. EVICTION. If the Rent called for in Section 4 of the Residential Rental Agreement is past due, then Owner shall have the right to evict Resident as set forth in Section 13 of the Residential Rental Agreement and terminate this Option to Purchase Agreement.

9. ATTORNEY'S FEES AND CLOSING COSTS. In any legal action to enforce any term under this Residential Rental Agreement, the prevailing party shall be entitled to all costs incurred in connection with such action, including reasonable attorney's fees and court costs. Upon Resident exercising its option to purchase under this Option to Purchase Agreement, Resident agrees to pay all closing costs, including attorney's fees, transfer fees, and recordation fees, in connection with the purchase of the Property.

10. WAIVER. No failure of Owner to enforce any term of this Option to Purchase Agreement shall be deemed a waiver.

In witness whereof, the parties hereto have caused this Option to Purchase Agreement to be signed in person or by a person duly authorized, on the day and year below. No modifications may be made to this Option to Purchase Agreement unless all parties agree in writing.

ACCEPTED AS WRITTEN THIS DATE _____

"MANAGEMENT"   **"RESIDENT"**

_____   _____

Marie Properties, LLC   **Danielle Scott/David Scott**
1234 Dennis Street
Diana, GA 30111

14

MANAGING LEASE/PURCHASE RELATIONSHIPS

You've spent a lot of time finding the right lease/ purchaser, and you're looking forward to a successful relationship. How do you get the relationship off on the right foot? How do you keep it on track? What about late payments? What's appropriate and what's not? This chapter will give you our thoughts based on some mistakes and plenty of successes.

SEPARATING BUSINESS FROM PERSONAL RELATIONSHIPS

We believe that one of the keys to your success will be your ability to manage your lease/purchase relationships as normal business relationships. This doesn't mean you can't be as honest, forthcoming, caring, and respectful as you are in your personal relationships. In fact, we believe these ingredients are important in all relationships, both business and personal.

However, because this relationship between you and your lease/ purchaser is fundamentally based on your real estate investment, your lease/purchaser must understand that if push comes to shove, your home comes first. This business relationship is especially tricky because you're dealing with people's *homes*, so the very nature of this business is personal. Yes, you want to build strong relationships with your lease/purchasers, but let them know that the business relationship takes precedence over the personal relationship. If you don't, your real estate business could suffer.

Dedicated Voice Mail for Your Real Estate Business

First, we suggest never giving out your home or work phone numbers. Get a phone number with voice mail so people can leave you messages when you're unavailable. This also keeps calls from coming into your residence, which can disturb you and your family at all hours of the day and night. If you have a day job, you can also maintain your real estate business without constant interruptions.

Dedicated Fax Number

We also highly recommend getting a dedicated fax number to support your real estate business. You will use it for communications with your lease/purchasers that require documentation but don't require originals (at least not immediately).

Dedicated Post Office Box

For privacy and security reasons, we strongly recommend never giving your home address to your lease/purchasers. We also encourage you to get a business post office box to separate your real estate business mail from your personal mail. This makes you look more professional. You should give out this address to your lease/purchasers (as well as the many others in your real estate network).

In the same way your lease/purchasers don't need to know where you live, they also don't need to know how much you owe on the home. Therefore, when you secure investment loans for your properties and fill out an address of record for the mortgage company, this address should be your post office box. However, no matter how careful you are, mortgage companies still sometimes send some documents to the property address (the home of the lease/purchaser). So, any time you purchase a property, fill out a change of address form with the post office. Then they will forward to your post office box any correspondence addressed to you at the property address.

Personal Liability Insurance Policy

Unlike your personal relationships, an additional element is the need for protection should the business relationship turn sour. Because this business has a lot of money on the line, it's possible a lease/purchaser (or someone else in your real estate network) could take you to court over some dispute. You should be able to obtain a personal liability policy from your insurance agent for $200 to $300 a year. That's in addition to having an insurance policy on each home protecting the property from damage. A personal liability policy protects you from injury or damage to the lease/purchaser or anyone else you do business with.

Be Careful with Promises

An unfulfilled promise in a business relationship could land you in court. Fortunately, we've never had to go to court to resolve a dispute affecting our real estate business. (Perhaps it's not "fortune" but more a function of our way of doing business.) You could be challenged by one of your lease/purchasers (either justifiably or not). Be aware of this threat and carefully monitor the promises you make.

Similarly, be careful about what you put in your written communications with your lease/purchasers. If you have *any* doubt that something you want to send to them via letter or fax could be used against you, spend the money necessary to have your real estate attorney review the wording. This holds true for your contracts, amendments, etc. One mistake could eat up a lot of your profits.

ESTABLISHING AND MAINTAINING RAPPORT

Good relationships are built over time. When establishing your relationships with your lease/purchasers, we recommend you spend as much time as you reasonably can getting to know each other. If you develop a good rapport with them, the odds improve significantly that they'll pay their rent on time, care for your home, and eventually purchase it from you. The lease/purchaser may also become a good reference for you and your program.

Communicate, Communicate, Communicate

Communicate, communicate, communicate may sound somewhat corny, but think about this. You have just made an investment in a nice home with a retail value of $100,000. You are talking to people you don't know and are considering trusting them with your investment. It's in your best interest to have a good feel for the people you are placing in your home. Any mistakes made in the selection process or problems later with the relationship can lead to headaches and financial losses in the months and years ahead.

After background checks and credit reports, the only really good way to get to know potential lease/purchasers is to *communicate* with them. Once they're in the home, the best way to keep the relationship on track is to continue to *communicate* with each other. Even after they purchase the home, you may want to ask them to be a reference for you, so *communicate* this, too.

We recommend engaging in thorough phone conversations during the initial contact. Introduce yourself and your lease/purchase program and try to get to know each other. We spend time talking with lease/purchase candidates when they view the home, when we go over the lease/purchase terms, when answering questions, and so on. Before making a selection, we talk again on the phone to make sure they understand the program and are still excited about the home. These conversations help all of us get to know each other and solidify the relationship. When it's time to sign the lease/purchase contract, we spend as much time as necessary talking with them about the terms of the agreement and making sure they're comfortable with the contract they are about to sign. We make ourselves further available to talk throughout the length of the lease/purchase agreement.

Be Straightforward and Honest

In the process of communicating, we hope it comes across that we're straightforward and honest people with no desire to deceive. We want to be transparent about how we run our real estate business, and we find transparency works to our advantage. Our objective has always been to be up front explaining how it operates, emphasizing that we're working toward our mutual benefit and following through on everything we promise. When we sense the candidate needs added confirmation that our program is everything we say it is—and that we are fair and honest people—we may have him or her contact current or former lease/purchasers for a reference. There absolutely is no better validation.

Being straightforward and honest at every step goes a long way in overcoming any fearful perception about lease/purchase programs, buying foreclosed properties, working with investors, and so on. It sets the tone for good long-term relationships.

Our 24-Hour Call-Back Rule

Regardless of where we are in the process with our lease/purchasers (or anyone else we are doing business with), we do our best to respond promptly to voice-mail messages. We follow the 24-hour call-back rule; that is, whenever we get a voice-mail message, we make a point of returning the call within 24 hours (with the exception of the initial callback).

Based on comments we have received, this practice has played a big role in establishing and maintaining credibility with our lease/purchasers (not to mention the members of our real estate team). Even when our schedules are hectic, we find time for a five- or ten-minute call—and that promptness makes a big difference. When we're on vacation, we have someone return calls on our behalf. If that's not possible, we leave a message on our voice mail about the date we'll return from our vacation.

The 24-hour call-back rule also helps build respect. Of course, lease/purchasers will hear from us (as they should expect to) if their rent is late. However, they also hear from us with the same degree of concern when they have an issue needing our attention. By showing the same attentiveness to issues concerning their well-being, we usually earn respect and receive similar treatment in return, which we believe has been a big factor in our success.

THE LITTLE EXTRAS

We recommend doing little extras to keep the relationship intact. For example, when stopping by the house to check on it (preferably once or twice a year), be sure to give advance notice. Take time to talk to your lease/purchasers and find out how they (and the house) are doing. You might also send them cards or small gifts during the December holiday season. This tells them you value the relationship.

THE SAVED MONEY LETTER

Another way to build trust and strengthen relationships is by sending a saved money letter each year. We send this letter out every January to remind our lease/purchasers how much money they've accumulated toward their down payment. The letter shows we are taking good care of their money and we're taking the relationship seriously.

Figure 14.1 shows an example of a saved money letter.

HANDLING LATE PAYMENTS

What is the universal, number one problem landlords deal with? Unquestionably, it's collecting rents on time. Certainly, chasing late payments has been our most common problem and will likely be yours, but that's expected since we typically work with people who are not in the best financial situations.

Therefore, we make sure they understand when the rent is due and overdue. For the most part, we don't let these dates slide, and we enforce the late fees. If we haven't received the rent check in our post office box by between the sixth and the eighth of the month, we usually call to find out where it is.

If you don't get the rent within a few days after the call, then you should send a notice of late rent letter. (See Figure 14.2.) This puts

FIGURE 14.1 *Saved Money Letter*

MAURICE PROPERTIES, LLC
P.O. BOX 8009
ATLANTA, GA 31986

January 25, 2004

Mark and Maya Schmid
3070 Carrie Lane
Roswell, GA 30597

Dear Mark and Maya,

As of December 31, 2003, for the property located at the above-referenced address, you have:

Accumulated Applied Rent....................	$2,100
Option Money...............................	$1,000
Security Deposit...........................	$ 995
Total	$4,095

If you have any questions, please feel free to give us a call at 404-123-4567.

Sincerely,

Andy Heller

lease/purchasers on notice that if they don't pay the month's rent and applicable late fees by a certain date, they must surrender the home or face a dispossessory (a notice from the county court essentially telling them to pay up or be in court on a certain date). If you don't get the rent within three to five days of sending the letter (you are now into the middle of the month), you should probably file a dispossessory at the local courthouse.

We're especially sensitive to the fact that when people get behind in their payments, they can dig themselves into a financial hole. Therefore, we highly recommend staying on top of calls, notice of late rent letters, and any dispossessory proceedings you may need to handle.

The Postman Usually Delivers

When we don't get rent payments on time, what happens if the post office really *is* at fault? The reality is, we've had a nearly 100 percent success rate receiving rent checks (and any other correspondence) through the mail in a timely manner. We can only remember a handful of times in all our years that the post office hasn't delivered (e.g., delivered a rent check to us on the 15th in an envelope postmarked on the 5th). Because mail delay is such a rare occurrence, it's not a big concern.

The additional security for everyone involved lies in the requirement of payment by cashier's checks or money orders. When we sign the lease/purchase, we tell the lease/purchaser that one of the reasons for cashier's checks and money orders is that, if there's ever an issue with a mail delay, they can show us receipts as validation that the rent payment was issued on a certain date and will likely arrive soon. If a rent payment is ever lost in the mail, those particular money orders and cashier's checks can be canceled and new ones reissued without financial penalty to us for the lease/purchaser.

Fax Copy of Cashier's Check

Whenever lease/purchasers are late sending the rent, we ask them to photocopy the cashier's check or money order for their rent payment (plus applicable late fee) and fax it over to us *the day* we call them about it and/or *the day* they receive the notice of late payment. This allows us to see that the check or money order for the rent and late fee has, in fact, been purchased. It gives us confidence that the money will really get to us in the next few days. And it overcomes the "check is in the mail" promise or excuse. If we haven't received the fax by 5:00 PM, we tell them we'll take the necessary steps to file a dispossessory.

Although we usually get the rent within a few days after receiving the fax, there is no guarantee they will mail it right after sending the fax. Fortunately, because the mail almost always comes within a few days, we know quickly if we have someone who is trying to pull one over on us. We have had creative lease/purchasers (fortunately, just a few) who wanted to buy more time by faxing us a copy of the rent check and late fee, and then going back to the place that issued the cashier's check or money order and getting their money back. This is why, if we don't get the rent in the mail within a few days, we usually file a dispossessory.

Special Exceptions

We recommend being consistent with your rent payment rules to encourage lease/purchasers to pay on time and minimize your headaches. However, you may choose to make a special exception from time to time. A first-time late payment or a death in the family may be grounds for waiving the late fee. However, a third late payment in a row or the excuse, "I had to make my car payment first," is not. Accept excuses rarely and infrequently; be careful and consistent with your rent payment rules.

When lease/purchasers can only make a partial payment, have them fax a letter stating the reason for being late and their plan to catch up. The letter usually forces them to take the matter more seriously, and it serves as a record of the situation in case they forget or you end up taking them to court. Make sure they follow through with their plan to pay you.

The Notice of Late Rent Letter

Whenever the lease/purchaser's rent is late and before filing a dispossessory, you should give the tenants notice that their rent is late and state what steps you plan to take. Figure 14.2 shows an example of a notice of late rent letter.

THE DISPOSSESSORY AND EVICTION

The dispossessory and eviction are powerful legal tools you may have to use from time to time. They should be used *carefully*. When used

FIGURE 14.2 *Example Notice of Late Rent Letter*

VIA CERTIFIED MAIL

NOTICE OF LATE RENT

Property: 1234 Lucille Street, Melvin, GA 30011
Residents: Rich and Tricia Singer
Date: October 10, 2003

A review of our records indicates that we have not received your rent for the month of October 2003 for the above-referenced property.

If we do not receive the sum............................$1,220
representing the unpaid rental in the amount of $1,195
plus late fees in the amount of $25

Within 24 hours of your receipt of this notice, a dispossessory warrant will be taken out and other necessary legal action will be taken to collect all money due on this claim (including the cost of the warrant and all court costs and attorney's fees), recover possession of the property, and exercise all other remedies provided by your lease agreement and by law.

The above amount must be paid in the form of cashier's check or money order and a copy faxed to 404-123-4567 and the original then immediately mailed. The amount stated above must be paid at management's address, shown below.

Notified by: Brian Frank
Management: Marcy Properties, LLC
Address: 5678 Ellen St., Barry, Georgia 30333

---

properly, the dispossessory can keep your lease/purchasers on track and positively affect your financial returns without negatively impacting your relationship with your good lease/purchasers. Dispossessory and evictions also vary from state to state, and may be referred to by different names.

Dispossessory versus Eviction

The filing of a dispossessory starts the legal process to obtain the rent you're owed (and getting your home back, if the lease/purchaser is unwilling to pay). The eviction physically removes them from the home.

In many states, the time between dispossessory filing and eviction is four to eight weeks.

Dispossessory filing costs vary from state to state (and can vary from county to county). In most states, filing costs less than $100 (depending on whether you hire an attorney or dispossessory company to help you). Evictions can cost several hundreds of dollars. You usually must pay for the time of a government official, such as a sheriff, and the eviction team to move the people's belongings out of the home and change the locks. The dispossessory and eviction usually can be canceled up to the last minute if the lease/purchaser gets current with the rent.

Despite variations from state to state, some forms of written notification are usually sent to the tenant from the court requiring them to pay up or come to court on a certain date. You can hire local law firms or companies who can file papers for a relatively small fee. We recommend checking with an attorney about the process in your state for dispossessory filings and evictions and become familiar with them.

Occasionally, a lease/purchaser can't come up with the full payment, and we agree to accept a portion of the rent. Check out the laws in your state concerning this; some states say if the landlord receives a partial payment, the tenant can't be kicked out for nonpayment of full rent. In our leases, we stipulate that a partial payment cannot be deemed a waiver of a full month's rent. (See Clause 19 of the Residential Rental Agreement in Chapter 13.)

As noted earlier, we deal with partial payment situations by having the lease/purchasers sign a paper stating how much they'll pay now and when they'll pay the remainder (stating a specific date). They then fax and mail this promissory note to us to document our verbal agreement to pay a split rent that month. Like every agreement, it must be specific and in writing.

The Pros and Cons of a Dispossessory

Most of the time, a dispossessory filing works well in keeping a good lease/purchaser out of trouble with our program, serving as a big wake-up call. If the people aren't destined to stay in your home, then the dispossessory begins a process that allows you to get the lease/purchaser to vacate the home sooner rather than later.

The only real downside with a dispossessory is that, from time to time, a lease/purchaser will take it personally when a sheriff pulls into their driveway to deliver the notice. Even though the rent was late and you made it clear that this was coming, they may claim to feel betrayed, embarrassed, and angry. However, the good lease/purchasers, because you have done everything reasonable to let them know what was coming, rarely get upset (and even then, our experience shows that these relationships can usually be mended). The bad lease/purchasers may be upset that you're about to end their free ride. They may even take out their anger on the home, leading to significant repair costs.

In our experience, most people can see a financial crunch coming. The reasonable (and realistic) lease/purchasers realize this and get out before the dispossessory process begins and almost always before the actual eviction takes place. In fact, we've had to deal with only one eviction in all these years—a track record that we believe, at least in part, can be attributed to our building good relationships and picking good lease/purchasers. Instead of wanting to milk us, good people tend to leave when their finances turn sour. They also realize an eviction is forthcoming and don't want to be around when the sheriff shows up. Believe it or not, there's a good chance they'll even leave the home in good condition because they have been treated fairly.

DEALING WITH LEASE/PURCHASER PROBLEMS

No one likes to get a letter, a call, or a notice about a problem with their home or lease/purchaser. However, it's great to have others keeping an eye on our properties to ensure the value of our home doesn't go down the tank. There can be a fine line between being soft and harsh on issues like this. Quite often, we base the judgment call on our gut instincts. We treat people with respect, while reminding them that they need to treat our home with respect (even though we don't use these exact words).

In the following real-life examples, you'll see how we have dealt with certain situations that you might face. In each case, we have tried to strike a balance between maintaining good relations with the lease/purchaser and taking good care of our real estate investment.

R e a l - L i f e E x a m p l e

THE CASE OF THE HOMEOWNERS ASSOCIATION LETTER

In this case, we received a letter from a homeowners association president concerning a family living in one of our homes. The letter claimed that our lease/purchaser had let the yard and outside paint deteriorate. We thought they were good lease/purchasers; they had always paid their rent on time and seemed serious about buying the home. We knew we had to find some way to make everyone happy.

Luckily, our arrangement with this family included a $5,000 improvement allowance that had not yet been used. We called them and suggested they use the allowance to pay for the yard repair and painting, which they did. If there had been no improvement allowance, we'd still have strongly encouraged them to take care of their responsibilities, as spelled out in the lease/purchase contract. If they had claimed they simply couldn't afford it, we might have fronted the money with a promissory note or added the costs of the work to the sales price of the home via an amendment to the lease/purchase contract.

For the lease/purchasers who pay their rent on time and take good care of our homes, we like to find a reasonable solution and work with them. After all, it's often more expensive for us to find new good lease/purchasers than to pay for landscaping and other repairs—and usually giving them a chance is also the right thing to do.

A n o t h e r R e a l - L i f e E x a m p l e

THE CASE OF THE NEIGHBOR'S CALL

In this situation, we received a call from a neighbor saying that the kids living in one of our homes were shooting BB guns around the neighborhood. Because we were on notice, we knew we could be liable for any injury from the BB guns. In this case, we called the parents (our lease/purchasers) and asked them to get rid of the BB guns. We also asked them to send us a letter to confirm they were gone, which they did. We kept their correspondence on file as proof we acted reasonably in case of future disputes.

THE CASE OF THE LOCAL ORDINANCE NOTICE

County officials sent us a letter about cars in the front yard of one of our homes. Parking on lawns was against the county ordinance. We contacted the family and asked them to remove the cars and confirm to us in writing that this had been done. We kept that letter on file as proof to the county that we were diligent, and we drove out to the property to confirm that the family had complied with the ordinance.

WHEN GOOD LEASE/PURCHASERS CAN'T BUY ON TIME

Every time we do a lease/purchase, we hope the people are able to buy the home within the time period of the option to purchase agreement. Unfortunately, some aren't able to do so before it expires. Possibly they need more time to improve their credit situation or save their down payment, or they might be hit by something unexpected like a death in the family or a job loss. Regardless of their situation, we do whatever we can to help them within reason, which most often is extending the lease/purchase agreement.

Rationale for a Fair Extension

Lease/purchasers are usually sitting on a gold mine because the home has appreciated in three years (in a stable economy), yet their purchase price hasn't gone up. In that length of time, they have also accumulated a substantial amount of money toward the down payment using our applied rent program. For example, if the applied rent is $150 a month and they've been paying for three years, they've saved up $5,400 plus their option money of, say, $1,000 (which they lose if they don't buy).

Remember, our goal is to keep the property lease/purchased with good and stable people in the home. This is a *basic premise* we live by in our real estate investment business. After all, we can lose a lot of money when no rent checks are coming in and we have to make repairs on the home. Therefore, we have a plan in place for these situations.

When to Grant an Extension

When we grant an extension (thus continuing our relationships with these lease/purchasers), here's what we look for.

- The lease/purchasers are honest and have communicated well with us.
- They have paid their rent on time most of the time.
- They're employed and have the financial means to keep the rent coming on time and potentially purchase the home.
- They want the house.

THE LEASE/PURCHASE EXTENSION AMENDMENT

The lease/purchase extension amendment gives the lease/purchasers additional time to get their finances, credit, etc., in order and lets them retain all applied rents they've accumulated.

During the first year of the extension, we normally leave the rent and purchase price unchanged. However, if the extension goes into two years or more, the rent and purchase price are increased by a modest amount, usually 2 to 3 percent a year. We're most proud of this part of our real estate program because it has allowed many good lease/purchasers to stay in our homes and eventually purchase them. It has also allowed us to save a lot of time and money by not having to lease/purchase these homes again.

Figure 14.3 shows an example of the lease/purchase extension amendment that has worked well for us.

FIGURE 14.3 *Example Lease/Purchase Extension Amendment*

LEASE/PURCHASE EXTENSION AMENDMENT

This agreement (hereinafter referred to as the "Amendment") is made between MARIE PROPER-TIES, LLC (hereinafter referred to as "Management/Owner") and DAVID and DIANA SCOTT (hereinafter referred to as "Resident") in connection with the Residential Rental Agreement and Option to Purchase Agreement dated July 31, 2005 (the "Lease/Purchase Agreement") for the property located at 246 Dennis Street, Danielle, GA 30078 (hereinafter referred to as the "Property").

1. TERM AND EXPIRATION. Section 1 of the Residential Rental Agreement and Section 1 of the Option to Purchase Agreement are hereby amended to automatically enter a period of one year renewals ("Renewal Periods") effective August 1, 2005, wherein Renewal Periods shall automatically continue for additional periods of one year unless either Management/Owner or Resident notifies the other in writing of its intent to terminate the Lease/Purchase Agreement at least ninety (90) days prior to the end of the then current Renewal Period.

2. MONIES PREVIOUSLY ACCUMULATED. Section 2B of the Option to Purchase Agreement is hereby amended so that all monies previously accumulated by Resident under the Option to Purchase Agreement shall still be available to Resident only if Resident chooses to exercise the Option to Purchase Agreement to purchase the Property. Otherwise all such monies previously accumulated shall be nonrefundable to Resident and shall immediately and automatically vest with Owner. After payment of July 2005 rent (assuming all rent payments are current), $5,595 shall be available to Resident toward Resident's purchase of the Property should Resident choose to exercise the Option to Purchase Agreement. The $5,595 represents $3,600 of Applied Rent plus $1,000 of Option Money plus $995 of Security Deposit.

3. FIRST RENEWAL PERIOD. Sections 4 and 5 of the Residential Rental Agreement and Sections 2A and 2B of the Option to Purchase Agreement are hereby amended so that in the first Renewal Period, the Rent and Purchase Price will remain unchanged. However, Management/Owner shall not apply any portion of the payments in connection with the Rent towards the purchase of the Property during this first Renewal Period.

4. SECOND AND FUTURE RENEWAL PERIODS. Sections 4 and 5 of the Residential Rental Agreement and sections 2A and 2B of the Option to Purchase Agreement are hereby amended so that, beginning with the second Renewal Period and for all Renewal Periods thereafter, the Rent and Purchase Price will increase by three percent (3%) per period over each prior period's Rent and Purchase Price amounts. However, Management will continue not to apply any portion of the payments in connection with the Rent toward the purchase of the Property during these Renewal Periods.

5. REMAINDER OF TERMS UNCHANGED. Management/Owner and Resident further acknowledge and agree that all other terms of the Lease/Purchase Agreement remain unchanged.

"MANAGEMENT/OWNER"　　**"RESIDENT"**　　　　**"RESIDENT"**

_____　_____　_____

MARIE PROPERTIES, LLC　**DAVID SCOTT**　　　　**DIANA SCOTT**

_____　_____　_____

Date　　　　　　　　　**Date**　　　　　　　　**Date**

NEED FOR FLEXIBILITY

We rarely deviate from our basic lease/purchase program. However, we have done so on a handful of occasions under some special circumstances, explained below.

Rent-Specific Situations

One example dealt with a married couple who had been paying $1,695 in rent and applying $200 of that toward the down payment. The $1,695 was a top rent for the property, and realistically, if we had to re-rent the property, a fair market rent at the time would have been $1,495 to $1,595. The wife had lost her job for three months, and then her husband had his wages garnished unexpectedly about four months later. They got behind on their payments and bounced a rent check—a red flag. They got further behind and, with late fees, were looking at a steep uphill climb to get caught up.

The good news was that they both began working again. They wanted to continue to lease/purchase the home, and we knew they were an honest, hardworking couple. After their two temporary setbacks, we decided to make an adjustment to the terms of the agreement. So we signed a lease/purchase amendment. For the next calendar year, they paid $1,495 in rent instead of $1,695, and we applied no portion of their rent toward their down payment during this year. The following year, they paid $1,595, and we applied $100 a month toward the down payment. In the third year, we went back to the original terms of $1,695 a month with $200 of applied rent. They haven't missed a beat paying the rent since, and it's been a win-win situation for all.

House-Specific Situations

One of our families wanted to have a fence in the backyard because of the family dog. As owners, we agreed to pay $1,000 toward building the fence and specified that the lease/purchasers pay that $1,000 when they eventually purchased the home. This arrangement was documented in a lease/purchase amendment. If they purchased the home, we'd get our $1,000 back (keeping a good lease/purchaser more than made up for the no-interest loan). If they didn't, we owned a fence for only $1,000.

A Word to the Wise

We all want to make people happy and keep the good lease/purchasers. Using lease/purchase amendments to build flexibility into our program can help achieve this. However, it's important to be very careful, especially with people who get behind on their rent payments. Sometimes it's simply best to get them out of the home and start fresh with a new lease/purchaser.

OUR PHILOSOPHY

A great benefit of our real estate program is the good people we get to know and develop relationships with. From the first contact we have, we do our best to be straightforward and honest. As we continue to get to know them, we try to show that we are dependable and caring. Of course, we pay close attention to identifying these same characteristics in the people we consider for our homes. We believe this approach has made an impact in the successful relationships we have enjoyed with most of our lease/purchasers and the resulting profits that have come our way.

Once people sign the lease/purchase contract, we continue to follow the Golden Rule—treat others as we'd like to be treated ourselves. We continue to be amazed at how this makes a big difference in people paying their rent on time, taking good care of our homes, purchasing them, and even moving out on good terms (if they are unable to pay their rent or purchase the home). It certainly feels good to positively affect people's lives and make more profits at the same time.

15

SELLING YOUR HOMES

You've learned how to buy low and how to rent smart. It's now time to complete the process and sell high. If you have spent a lot of time finding good properties, fixing them up, and attracting good lease/purchasers, why should you sell? You have entered into a lease/purchase agreement, so what do you do when your tenants notify you of their intent to buy? What do you do when your lease/purchase marketing attracts someone who actually wants to strictly purchase your property? This chapter answers these questions and more.

A KEY COMPONENT TO GENERATING REAL ESTATE WEALTH

Earlier, we outlined six different ways we realize a profit using our real estate investment model. Recall the first profit source:

We buy homes at a 10 to 20 percent discount of their current market value. By acquiring them at below-market prices, we realize a profit at the time of sale by selling the homes at the fair market value.

Although the other profit sources play key roles in our model, the sale is the most significant. It allows you, the investor, to generate a substantial cash windfall, while the other sources grow your cash at a slower, steadier pace. If you are reinvesting profits (rather than removing them from your real estate business), you'll be effectively increasing your cash position, thus reducing your dependency on borrowed funds and the cost of interest. Each sale can move you closer to all-cash purchasing, followed by refinancing to replenish your cash. These all-cash purchases also open up deals and discounts not available when offers are contingent on securing outside financing. (See Chapter 5, "Money for Purchasing Your Homes.")

There are the two primary ways of selling your properties using our model: lease/purchase and outright sale. Both allow you to sell at the fair market value (little or no discount) and cut out real estate commissions (which can drain your profits). Because you want to sell at little or no discount plus get the cash flowing fast, you'll sell most of your homes using the lease/purchase format. However, from time to time, you'll get an offer to purchase your home outright at or close to fair market value.

THE LEASE/PURCHASE SALE

This sale is the ultimate win-win scenario. You, the investor, make a healthy profit, while providing a helping hand to people who need it to realize their dream of home ownership. Actual results vary from community to community, but we've found that one-third to one-half of our lease/purchasers actually buy the homes.

Many lease/purchasers who don't buy live in our homes as tenants for extended periods. Their rent increases 2 to 3 percent a year after the expiration of the original lease/purchase agreement. Remember, one of our rules is *never* to kick out a lease/purchaser who is taking good care of the property and making timely payments. Some move out for such reasons as job transfer, change in family size, change in income level, etc. If they move out on good terms (i.e., the rent is current and the house is in good condition), we simply refund the security deposit and keep their option money. Then we do a marketing study to determine appreciation in the neighborhood, establish new rental and sale prices, and lease/purchase the home again.

Getting Ready for Closing

When your lease/purchasers tell you they want to exercise their purchase option, congratulate them. Often, these people have overcome major financial obstacles and deserve a lot of praise. For you, they become excellent references, plus you can feel good about helping them realize their goal.

The rest is simply logistics. You have a pending sale with a purchase price that has been agreed to months and often years earlier. There is no inspection clause that can hang up the deal, because the purchaser has been living in the property for an extended period of time and knows it well. So you find out the name of the mortgage company and closing attorney, and fax or e-mail them an option to purchase sales summary (see below). This summary simplifies the option to purchase agreement for the attorney. Many attorneys have never seen anything like our lease/purchase program before, so be diligent with the details. It's not uncommon for closing attorneys to make an error involving a program that's unfamiliar to them.

After submitting the summary, the next steps are to set the date, time, and place for the closing. Then show up to sign over ownership of the home to the lease/purchaser and deposit a large check into your bank account.

Option to Purchase Sales Summary

Figure 15.1 shows an example of an option to purchase sales summary for a home with a fixed sales price of $169,900, option money of $1,500, applied rent of $150/month, and a security deposit of $1,695. We'll assume the lease/purchaser has lived in the home for 18 months.

THE STRAIGHT SALE

While most of your homes will eventually sell to lease/purchasers, we recommend you welcome offers from strict purchasers. After all, in marketing your homes, you are using the term *lease/purchase* and advertising in the "For Sale" section of the newspaper. Therefore, you will get inquiries from those strictly seeking to purchase.

FIGURE 15.1 *Example Option to Purchase Sales Summary*

Option to Purchase Sales Summary for:

1234 Carrie Drive
Barbara, GA 30303
Seller: Andy Heller
Buyer: Matt and Cindy Schwartz

Dear Closing Attorney,

The following are the specifics for the sale of the above-referenced property.

- *Sales Price.* $169,900
- *Option Money.* $1,500, to be applied towards down payment
- *Applied Rent.* $150/month × 18 months of tenancy = $2,700 (to be applied toward down payment)
- *Security Deposit.* $1,695 (to be applied towards down payment)
- Buyer to pay all closing costs

The loan on the property is held by Marc Tepper Mortgage Company, 800-123-4567, loan #123456, and the seller's Social Security number is 987-65-4321.

If you have questions, please do not hesitate to call the seller at 404-222-1777.

Sincerely,

Andy Heller

For these situations, you may receive an offer below your fair market value asking price. Unless you can get an offer or counteroffer to within 5 percent of your asking price (for example, $95,000 on a home for which you're asking $99,900), then we suggest you pass. After all, by keeping and lease/purchasing the home, you will likely be able to sell the home for your full asking price (the fair market value) *and* access the other five profit sources.

You may wonder why you should do a straight sale with a 5 percent discount when you can get fair market value later and access our other profit sources now. It's because, Cash Is King. More cash on hand sooner allows you to buy more homes sooner, so selling at a slight discount can help you generate wealth faster. Also, remember that you purchased the home at a 10 to 20 percent discount, so $10,000 cash profit on $100,000 (purchased at $85,000 and sold at $95,000) is not too shabby for a few months of part-time work.

Negotiating with Strict Purchasers

Does the lease/purchase emphasis in your marketing hurt your ability to straight sell (flip) properties for close to fair market value? Probably not. In fact, the lease/purchase format actually *helps* maximize the sales price when a strict purchaser shows interest by giving you leverage in the negotiations.

Here's how. We explain to our potential strict purchasers that our ultimate goal is to sell the home. However, one reason we use the lease/purchase format is to maximize the return on our investment, because we generally find a good lease/purchaser in a few weeks and set a sales price at fair market value. We'll gladly wait up to three years to realize our full profit as a trade-off for selling at fair market value and minimizing our holding costs.

Effectively, the purchaser's competition is the potential lease/purchase you can enter into quickly for fair market value. If the strict purchaser wants the home and you have explained the lease/purchase program well, that person often makes a fair offer and makes it quickly. If that buyer still wants a discount that's too steep, you can simply say you prefer to hold on to the property and find a lease/purchaser who will pay the fair market value. Realizing this, many purchasers increase their offers to a level that's acceptable, allowing you to close the deal.

Using a Standard Real Estate Purchase Contract

For straight sales, the offer will usually be made in the form of a standard real estate purchase contract used by the local real estate association. We suggest you obtain one from a local real estate agent before marketing your property. You can get familiar with it, and it may come in handy if the buyer doesn't already have one. Remember, the real estate purchase contract we use for buying contains special provisions (explained in Chapter 8, "The Real Estate Purchase Contract") to protect you, the buyer/investor, when dealing with sophisticated lenders (banks and mortgage companies). However, when you sell, you don't want these special buyer provisions to be in the contract, and the local real estate association contract should be fair to all involved (both to you and a less sophisticated buyer).

Working with the Buyer's Real Estate Agent

Occasionally, you'll receive an offer from a purchaser represented by a buyer's real estate agent. This real estate agent is likely expecting a standard real estate commission (3 to $3\frac{1}{2}$ percent in many communities). This fee may be enough to turn an acceptable offer into an unacceptable one. For example, a house that cost you $85,000 and that you're marketing for $99,900 carries a potential profit of $14,900. If a strict purchaser offers $95,000 without an agent, then a profit of $10,000 is not bad for two months' work. However, if a strict purchaser makes a higher offer of $96,000, with a $3\frac{1}{2}$ percent real estate commission attached, this offer actually nets out at $92,640. That's $7,640 in profits—considerably less attractive. Involving a real estate agent often makes the deal unworkable—but not always, as this story illustrates.

R *e a l - L i f e* E *x a m p l e*

A purchaser came to us with a buyer's agent. We quickly determined that he was serious and wanted the home, yet after factoring in a discount coupled with the agent's commission, his offer wasn't attractive to us. It seemed to make more sense to continue marketing the home. We then put all three parties together on the phone: us (the seller), the buyer, and the buyer's agent. We explained that with the price discount *and* the real estate agent's commission, the offer was unattractive so we decided to seek a lease/purchaser who would pay fair market value with no real estate sales commission. We said the only way to make the deal work was for all three parties to give a little.

So here's what we did. We agreed to a reasonable discount off of the fair market value; we asked the buyer to pay more than intended; we suggested the agent accept a discounted commission. In sum, we all chipped in a third of the difference. Nobody got exactly what they wanted, but with these compromises, the result was an acceptable deal for all concerned.

The lesson is that a compromise might enable you to flip a property even when an agent is involved. Because placing buyers in homes they are happy with takes a lot of time and effort, many agents won't risk walking away from a satisfactory deal due to a squabble over commission. In addition, the agreement between agent and buyer is for a limited duration. If an agent can't find a home for the buyer within the specified period, he or she runs the risk of losing the client and earning absolutely nothing. So, by offering a compromise *and* respecting the agent's investment in time and effort, the idea of a reasonably reduced commission has a good chance of being accepted.

Four Do Nots

Here are some additional rules of thumb to follow when considering straight sales.

1. *Do not* consider any offers from purchasers who cannot present, with their offer, a prequalification letter—a letter from an established mortgage company that shows that the buyer is prequalified for a loan to purchase your home.
2. *Do not* seriously consider any offer until it's presented in writing and you've received earnest money of 1 to 2 percent of the sales price. In fact, we recommend this standard response to any interested queries: "We would be happy to consider your offer to purchase, but we will continue to market our home for lease/purchase until we receive an acceptable offer to purchase in writing accompanied by a prequalification letter and earnest money." Don't just say this; *do* it. Under no circumstances should you withdraw your marketing until you have an acceptable offer in writing with appropriate earnest money.
3. *Do not* remove your sign from the front of the home until the home closes. Even consider keeping your ad running in the paper until the home actually closes. This is your call and consideration should be given to the cost of the ad. It's good "insurance" to continue receiving qualified inquiries in case the purchase falls through before closing, yet this insurance comes with a price. If you have a good feeling about the purchaser's ability to close, any advertising that costs more than a few hundred dollars may be overkill.

If you do choose to withdraw your advertising, we suggest doing so only *after* the purchaser's property inspection, which usually takes place within ten days of an accepted contract. You may have an acceptable offer, but after the inspection, the purchaser can counter with unreasonable requests and your deal collapses. The probability of a purchase contract falling through is considerably reduced after the home inspection has been completed and the seller and buyer have reached agreement on any issues.

4. *Do not* seriously consider offers with extra provisions that can leave you holding the bag. Examples include: 60 days to close rather than the standard 30 days; a purchase contingent on the buyer selling his or her home (i.e., buyer doesn't have a firm contract pending on the current home); "wild" financing contingencies; additional significant, prepurchase, seller-financed repairs; etc.

OUR PHILOSOPHY

Selling some of your properties periodically is important to growing your wealth with real estate. Selling properties at fair market value (selling high) allows you to pull cash out of your properties, which can be reinvested in more homes purchased at a discount (buying low).

We favor the lease/purchase format because it allows you to obtain fair market value sales prices for your homes *consistently*. It also allows you to tap into the six profit sources while waiting for lease/purchasers to exercise their options to purchase.

However, if you get fair market value (or very close to it) from a straight purchase, we encourage you to consider the offer seriously. After all, getting your cash windfall sooner, while still selling high, lets you reinvest in more homes and grow both your real estate business and your wealth faster.

FINAL THOUGHTS

When we made the decision to write this book, we were excited to share our program of real estate investing that is rewarding beyond the profits it generates. Many of the relationships we've established with people on our real estate team and our lease/purchasers have lasted a long time, and the wealth we've built from our real estate business should last us a lifetime.

Now that our program is set out in this book, we hope you can use it to achieve your own financial and relationship successes. Our approach is not a get-rich-quick scheme. Rather, it's a longer-term, sustainable vehicle to an American Dream—achieving financial freedom. Our approach also allows you to help many good people who have been thrown life-changing curveballs or have simply made financial mistakes and need help to make another American Dream come true—owning a home. *This program provides deserving people with a transition step between renting and home ownership, while allowing you to make a fair and attractive profit along the way.*

We wish you the best of luck as you begin your journey on this exciting road to financial independence and long-lasting relationships.

S *ample* POTENTIAL INVESTMENT HOME CHECKLIST

S *ample* REAL ESTATE PURCHASE CONTRACT FOR BUYING HOMES

S *ample* COVER LETTER FOR BUYING HOMES

S *ample* HOME INSPECTION CHECKLIST

S *ample* LEASE/PURCHASE ADVERTISEMENT IN LOCAL NEWSPAPER

S *ample* LEASE/PURCHASE FLYER

S *ample* LEASE/PURCHASE SIGN FOR FRONT YARD

S *ample* APPLICATION TO LEASE/PURCHASE HOME

S *ample* EMPLOYMENT VERIFICATION FORM

S *ample* TENANCY VERIFICATION FORM

S *ample* LEASE AGREEMENT

S *ample* OPTION TO PURCHASE AGREEMENT

S *ample* SAVED MONEY LETTER

S *ample* NOTICE OF LATE RENT LETTER

S *ample* LEASE/PURCHASE EXTENSION AMENDMENT

S *ample* OPTION TO PURCHASE SALES SUMMARY

SAMPLE POTENTIAL INVESTMENT HOME CHECKLIST

Note: For more details on how to use this, refer to Chapter 6, "Finding Good Homes."

Date Property Seen ____/____/____

Address _____ Price _____ Down Pmt. _____

BR ___ BA ___ GAR ___ Prob. Rent _____

Seller _____ Phone _____

Age ____ yrs. Neighborhood _____ 1- or 2-story _____ Driveway _____

Exterior: Roof _____ Landscape _____ Paint _____ Trees _____

Front Yard _____ Back Yard _____ Fenced _____

Porch _____ Patio _____ Deck _____ Shed _____ Other _____

Den: Fireplace _____ Walls _____ Carpet _____ Ceiling _____

Size _____ OH Light _____ Ceiling Fan _____ Other _____

Dining Room: Attached _____ Walls _____ Carpet _____ Ceiling _____

Size _____ OH Light _____ Ceiling Fan _____ Other _____

Kitchen: Size _____ Walls _____ Floor _____ Stove/Dish./Fridge _____

Pantry _____ Cabinets _____ Ceiling _____ Other _____

Garage: Size _____ Opener _____ Shelves _____ Other _____

Hallway: Walls _____ Carpet _____ Linen Closet _____ Other _____

Laundry Room: Location _____ Size _____ Other _____

Master Bedroom: Size _____ Walls _____ Carpet _____ Ceiling _____

Closet _____ OH Light _____ Ceiling Fan _____ Other _____

1st Bedroom: Size _____ Walls _____ Carpet _____ Ceiling _____

Closet _____ OH Light _____ Ceiling Fan _____ Other _____

2nd Bedroom: Size _____ Walls _____ Carpet _____ Ceiling _____

Master Bath: Size _____ Walls _____ Floor _____ Pressure _____ Other _____

Hall Bath: Size _____ Walls _____ Floor _____ Pressure _____ Other _____

Rentals in Neighborhood:

Address _____ Phone _____ Size _____ Rent _____ Sec. Dep. _____

Address _____ Phone _____ Size _____ Rent _____ Sec. Dep. _____

Address _____ Phone _____ Size _____ Rent _____ Sec. Dep. _____

For Sale in Neighborhood:

Address _____ Phone _____ Size _____ Price _____ Terms _____

Address _____ Phone _____ Size _____ Price _____ Terms _____

Address _____ Phone _____ Size _____ Price _____ Terms _____

SAMPLE REAL ESTATE PURCHASE CONTRACT FOR BUYING HOMES

Note: For more details on how to use this, refer to Chapter 8, "The Real Estate Purchase Contract."

REAL ESTATE PURCHASE CONTRACT

1. PURCHASE AND SALE. The undersigned purchaser agrees to buy, and the undersigned seller agrees to sell, all that tract of land, with such improvements as are located thereon, described as follows: The house known as _____
according to the present system of numbering. Together with all lighting fixtures attached thereto, all electrical, mechanical, plumbing, air-conditioning, and any other systems or fixtures as are attached thereto; all television antennae and mailboxes; and all plants, trees, and shrubbery now a part of the property. The full legal description of said property is the same as is recorded with the clerk of the superior court of the county in which the property is located and is made a part of this agreement by reference.

2. PURCHASE PRICE AND METHOD OF PAYMENT. The purchase price of the property shall be: _____ dollars. Purchase is contingent on purchaser obtaining an investor loan at ___% down payment with an interest rate not to exceed ___% on a ___-year loan.

3. EARNEST MONEY. Purchaser has paid to the undersigned seller $_____ (check), receipt whereof is hereby acknowledged as earnest money, and is to be applied as part of payment of purchase price of said property at the time of closing. Purchaser and seller agree that the seller shall deposit earnest money in the seller's account by the third banking day following acceptance of this agreement by all parties; all parties have agreed that said escrow/ trust account will be an interest-bearing account, with interest also applied to the purchase price at time of closing. The parties to this contract understand and acknowledge that disbursement of earnest monies held by escrow agent can occur only at closing; upon written agreement signed by all parties having an interest in the funds; upon court order; or upon failure of loan approval; or as otherwise set out herein. This contract is voidable at seller's option if the earnest money check is not paid when presented to the drawee bank.

4. WARRANTY OF TITLE. Seller warrants that he presently has title to said property, and at the time of closing, he agrees to convey good and marketable title to said property to purchaser by general warranty deed subject only to (1) zoning ordinances affecting said property, (2) general utility easements of record serving said property, (3) subdivision restrictions of record, and (4) leases, other easements, other restrictions, and encumbrances specified in this contract.

5. TITLE EXAMINATION. The purchaser shall have a reasonable time after acceptance of this contract to examine the title and furnish seller with a written statement of objections affecting the marketability of said title. Seller shall have a reasonable time after receipt of such

(continued)

objections to satisfy all valid objections, and if seller fails to satisfy such valid objections within a reasonable time, then at the option of the purchaser, evidenced by written notice to seller, this contract shall be null and void. Marketable title as used herein shall mean title which a title insurance company licensed to do business in the state of Georgia will insure at its regular rates, subject only to standard exceptions unless otherwise specified herein.

6. DESCRIPTION OF PREMISES. Seller warrants that at the time of closing the premises will be in the same condition as it is on the date that this contract is signed by the seller, normal wear and tear excepted. However, should the premises be destroyed or substantially damaged before time of closing, then at the election of the purchaser: (a) the contract may be canceled, (b) the purchaser may consummate the contract and receive such insurance as is paid on the claim of loss. This election is to be exercised within 10 days after the purchaser has been notified in writing by seller of the amount of the insurance proceeds, if any, seller will receive on the claim of loss. If purchaser has not been so notified within 45 days, subsequent to the occurrence of such damage or destruction, purchaser may, at its option, cancel the contract.

7. RESPONSIBILITY TO COOPERATE. Seller and purchaser agree that such documents as may be necessary to carry out the terms of this contract shall be produced, executed, and/or delivered by such parties at the time required to fulfill the terms and conditions of this agreement.

SPECIAL STIPULATIONS

1. REAL ESTATE TAXES. Real estate taxes on said property for the calendar year in which the sale is closed shall be prorated as of the date of closing.

2. STATE TRANSFER TAX. Seller shall pay state of _____ property transfer tax.

3. CLOSING DATE AND COSTS. Sale shall be closed on or before _____ at such time, date, and location specified by seller. Seller shall pay all closing costs in connection with the sale of subject property to purchaser.

4. UTILITY BILL PRORATED. Seller and purchaser agree to prorate between themselves, as of the date of closing, any and all utility bills rendered subsequent to closing which include service for any period of time the property was owned by the seller or any prior owner.

5. WOOD-INFESTATION REPORT. At the time of closing seller shall provide purchaser with a wood-destroying infestation report, in the current form officially approved by _____ structural pest control commission, from a properly licensed pest control company stating that the main dwelling has been inspected and found to be free of visible infestation and structural damage caused by termites and other wood-destroying organisms or that if such infestation or structural damage existed it has been corrected. The inspection referred to in such report shall have been made within 30 days prior to closing. The inspection and termite letter is to be provided by _____.

6. SURVIVAL OF TERMS OF CONTRACT. Any condition or stipulation of the contract not fulfilled at the time of closing shall survive the closing, execution, and delivery of the warranty deed until such time as said conditions or stipulations are fulfilled. ** Closing attorney is directed to transfer this paragraph to the closing statement.

7. SEWER/SEPTIC TANK. Seller warrants that the main dwelling on the above described property is served by:

    * A PUBLIC SEWER _____ OR BY

    * A SEPTIC TANK _____

                 (PURCHASER) (SELLER)

8. WALK-THROUGH AND INSPECTION. Purchaser has the right to walk through the property and to have an inspection of the premises made by a qualified building inspector within 10 business days of acceptance of this contract. Expense of the inspection shall be paid by the purchaser. Should purchaser present to seller within this 10-day period a report citing any deficiencies in the property found during the walk-through or inspection, seller, at his option, may elect to correct said deficiencies, request purchaser to accept "as is," or allow purchaser to declare contract null and void. Seller shall have 48 hours to decide which repairs, if any, are to be made. Purchaser shall have 48 hours after notice from seller to accept seller's offer of repairs or declare contract null and void.

    This instrument shall be regarded as an offer by the purchaser or seller who first signs to the other and is open for acceptance by the other until _____ PM on the _____ day of _____ by which time written acceptance of such offer must have been actually received by _____. Acceptance can be communicated this week to _____ at:

    FAX: _____

    PHONE: _____

THE ABOVE PROPOSITION IS HEREBY ACCEPTED, _____ O'CLOCK ____M., THIS _____ DAY OF_____, _____

PURCHASER _____, HEIRS AND/OR ASSIGNS

PURCHASER ADDRESS

SELLER

SELLER ADDRESS

SAMPLE COVER LETTER FOR BUYING HOMES

Note: For more details on how to use this, refer to Chapter 8, "The Real Estate Purchase Contract."

Andy Heller
P.O. Box 1234
Atlanta, GA 30000
Tel: 770-547-3479
Fax: 770-548-9761

DATE :   October 8, 2003
TO   :   Rachel Teisch—Teisch Realty (REO Agent)
FROM :   Andy Heller
RE   :   2846 David Street, Jonesboro, GA 32005

John, the following is my offer, summarized below, on 2846 David Street. This home has a lot of potential. However, I wish to emphasize a few key points.

First, this subdivision has shown a small drop in sales prices during the past year. It's not huge but worth noting. Second, this house is a three-bedroom with office, *not* a four-bedroom as advertised. The fourth room is simply not a functional bedroom (no closet).

The house will need approximately $20,000 in repairs/improvements. All flooring will need to be replaced, interior painting needs to be done, kitchen appliances are missing, a new master prefab shower is needed, the garage door will probably need replacement, some new siding is needed, and water damage is worse than originally thought. In addition, there is some concern the HVAC system may be on its last legs.

Terms:

- Offer $100,000
- Purchase as is (subject to thorough inspection within ten days of acceptance)
- Closing within 30 days
- Termite letter required. If not already done, please arrange to be provided by Nopest Termites, contact Bob Hightower at 770-367-6434.

Warmest regards,

Andy Heller

SAMPLE HOME INSPECTION CHECKLIST

Note: For more details on this, refer to Chapter 9, "Fixing Up Your Homes."

Home Inspection Checklist for

_____

Room	Problem Item	Specific Problem

_____   _____   _____   _____

Management   Date   Resident   Date

SAMPLE LEASE/PURCHASE ADVERTISEMENT IN LOCAL NEWSPAPER

Note: For more details on this, refer to Chapter 11, "Marketing Your Homes."

ATLANTA By Owner

LEASE/PURCHASE

4 br, 2.5 ba, 2-car gar, big fenced backyard,

completely updated, incredible terms, applied rent

$119,900 $1,195/mo   404-123-4567

SAMPLE LEASE/PURCHASE FLYER

Note: For more details on this, refer to Chapter 11, "Marketing Your Homes."

1234 DIANA STREET
MARIE, GA 30319

LEASE/PURCHASE

- *4 bedrooms*
- *2½ bathrooms*
- *2-car garage*
- *fantastic location*
- *cul-de-sac living*
- *master with garden tub and separate shower*
- *completely updated*
- *large basement*
- *ask us about $5,000 improvement allowance*

Schools: David Elementary
           Danielle Middle School
           Dennis High School

INCREDIBLE TERMS

$1,495/month . . . $150 applied rent per month
$149,900 purchase with up to 3 years to close
$1,495 security deposit
$1,500 option money

Questions call Scott at 404-123-4567

SAMPLE LEASE/PURCHASE SIGN FOR FRONT YARD

Note: For more details on this, refer to Chapter 11, "Marketing Your Homes."

SAMPLE APPLICATION TO LEASE/PURCHASE HOME

Note: For more details on this, refer to Chapter 12, "Finding the Right Lease/Purchasers."

RESIDENTIAL PROPERTY LEASE APPLICATION

This application will be processed and rated. Any omission or incorrect information may lead to a delay or refusal of leasing of property. Purposeful presentation of false or misleading information can result in removal from said premises by the landlord at anytime. Thank you.

Name (1st adult) _____ Social Security Number ___-__-____ Date of Birth __/__/__

Marital Status: Single Divorced Married   Spouse's Name _____

Home Phone (_____) _____-_____   Work Phone (_____) _____-_____

Name (2nd adult) _____ Social Security Number ___-__-____ Date of Birth __/__/__

Home Phone (_____) _____-_____   Work Phone (_____) _____-_____

Name of anyone else who will be occupying this property

1) Name _____ Relationship _____ Age ___

2) Name _____ Relationship _____ Age ___

3) Name _____ Relationship _____ Age ___

Residence for last 3 years (list present residence first)

1) Street Address _____ Apt. # ___ City _____ State ___

Name of apartments, leasing office, or property owner _____

Phone Number (_____) _____-_____ Dates lived there from: __/__/__ to: __/__/__

Rent per month $_____

Reason for leaving _____

2) Street Address _____ Apt. # ___ City _____ State ___

Name of apartments, leasing office, or property owner _____

Phone Number (_____) _____-_____ Dates lived there from: __/__/__ to: __/__/__

Rent per month $_____

Reason for leaving _____

3) Street Address _____ Apt. # ___ City _____ State ___

Name of apartments, leasing office, or property owner _____

Phone Number (_____) _____-_____ Dates lived there from: __/__/__ to: __/__/__

Rent per month $_____

Reason for leaving _____

(continued)

Employment for last 3 years (list present job first)

1) Name of Company _____ Address _____

Position held _____ Monthly income _____ Supervisor_____

Phone number_____ Dates employed from: ___/___/___ to: ___/___/___

2) Name of Company _____ Address _____

Position held _____ Monthly income _____ Supervisor_____

Phone number_____ Dates employed from: ___/___/___ to: ___/___/___

3) Name of Company _____ Address _____

Position held _____ Monthly income _____ Supervisor_____

Phone number_____ Dates employed from: ___/___/___ to: ___/___/___

Credit References

1) Bank or Credit Card _____ Account Number_____ Monthly Payment _____

Balance _____ Phone Number_____ Contact Person _____

2) Bank or Credit Card _____ Account Number_____ Monthly Payment _____

Balance _____ Phone Number_____ Contact Person _____

Do you own any pets? ___ If so, how many? ___ If so, what types? _____

If not, do you plan on getting any, and if so, what types? _____

A nonrefundable charge of $25 is required for processing this application. Acceptance of application and application fee deposited herewith are not binding upon Landlord.

I/We certify that the information given herein is complete, true, and correct. This application must be signed before it can be processed. Any false information constitutes grounds for rejection of application.

How soon would you like to move in? ____   _____ ___/___/___

                                          Signature of Applicant   Date

_____, IS HEREBY AUTHORIZED TO INVESTIGATE THIS APPLICATION AND OBTAIN A CREDIT REPORT FOR REVIEW BY LANDLORD.

SAMPLE EMPLOYMENT VERIFICATION FORM

Note: For more details on this, refer to Chapter 12, "Finding the Right Lease/Purchasers."

DATE: _____

TO: _____

Fax: _____

FROM: _____

Phone: _____

Fax: _____

RE: Employment Verification for _____

Number of pages including cover ____

Following is the signed lease application for the above-referenced employee. Please verify length of employment as well as present monthly salary. Any additional information would be appreciated. Please feel free to call me at _____ to discuss or, if you respond in writing, to fax the information to me at _____. Thank you for your time.

Sincerely,

_____

SAMPLE TENANCY VERIFICATION FORM

Note: For more details on this, refer to Chapter 12, "Finding the Right Lease/Purchasers."

DATE: _____

TO: _____
           Fax: _____

FROM: _____
           Phone: _____
           Fax: _____

RE: Tenancy Verification for _____

Number of pages including cover _____

Please verify tenancy for the above-mentioned tenant. Following is a signed application from this prospective tenant. We are seeking verification of basic information:

Number of months as a tenant _____

Number of times tenant paid late _____

Please give details on late payments (how late, explanations) _____

Is this tenant current with the rent? _____

Is this tenant required to provide notice before moving out? _____

If notice is required, how many days in advance? _____

Please feel free to call me at _____ to discuss or, if you respond in writing, to fax the information to me at _____. Thank you for your time.

Sincerely,

_____

SAMPLE LEASE AGREEMENT

Note: For more details on this, refer to Chapter 13, "The Lease/Purchase Contract."

RESIDENTIAL RENTAL AGREEMENT

This agreement (hereinafter referred to as the "Residential Rental Agreement") is made this _____ between _____ (hereinafter referred to as "Management") and _____ (hereinafter referred to as "Resident"). Management leases to Resident and Resident rents from Management, the residential property located at _____ (hereinafter referred to as the "Property" and the "Premises"), under the following conditions:

1. TERM. The term of this Residential Rental Agreement shall be ___ months, beginning Noon, _____, and ending Noon, _____.

2. POSSESSION. If there is a delay in the possession of the Property to Resident by Management, Rent (as set forth in Section 4) shall be abated on a daily basis until possession is granted. If possession is not granted within seven (7) days after the beginning of the term, Resident may void the Residential Rental Agreement and have a full refund of any Rent or Security Deposit (as set forth in Section 7) already paid Management. However, Management shall not be liable for damages resulting from the delay of possession.

3. OCCUPANCY. It is specifically understood and agreed that the Resident represents that the family unit consists of _____ (__) adults and _____ (__) children, and that at no time will the Resident permit guests, visitors, or others to reside on the Premises for any extended period of time, and in no event in excess of fourteen (14) days without having obtained the prior written consent of Management.

4. RENT. Rent is payable monthly, in advance and in full, at a rate of _____ ($_____) per month, during the term of this Residential agreement on the fifth (5th) day of each month (the "Rent Due Date") at Management's address as set forth below or at such other place as may be designated by Management from time to time. Rent shall increase at a rate of ___ percent (__%) every year beginning on _____.

5. DISCOUNT RENT. If the Rent is received by Management before 5:00 PM of the first (1st) day of the month, the Rent will be discounted One Hundred Dollars ($100) to Nine Hundred _____ ($___) (the "Discount Rent"). The Discount Rent is to increase at a rate of ___ percent (__%) every year beginning on _____.

6. LATE FEES AND RETURNED CHECK FEES. Time is of the essence. If the Rent is not paid by the fifth (5th) day of the month, Resident shall pay Management Five Dollars ($5) per day as late fee for each day that the Rent shall remain unpaid. Each daily failure to pay such additional late charge shall be a separate event of default. In the event any check given to

(continued)

Management by Resident is returned by the bank unpaid, Resident shall pay a returned check fee of Fifty Dollars ($50) for each check returned unpaid in addition to the aforementioned daily late fees, with all subsequent monies due and payable in certified funds.

7. SECURITY DEPOSIT. Resident shall pay Management a deposit of _____ Dollars ($____) (the "Security Deposit") to be held by Management as a security for the faithful performance of the terms of this Residential Rental Agreement to be held in Account # _____ in _____ Bank, where any interest accruing on the Security Deposit will become the property of Management. At the termination of this lease, the Security Deposit may be used by Management to pay for any damages to property (beyond ordinary wear and tear), and the expense of cleaning, if the property is vacated in an unclean condition. Resident shall not apply the Security Deposit in payment of any month's rent, including the last month's rent, unless Resident has obtained prior written consent from Management. Nothing in this Residential Rental Agreement shall preclude Management from retaining the Security Deposit for nonpayment of rent or of fees, for the abandonment of the Premises, for nonpayment of utility charges, for repair work or cleaning contracted by Resident with a third party, or for actual damages caused by Resident's breaching this Residential Rental Agreement. The balance, if any, of the Security Deposit shall be refunded to Resident within thirty (30) days after termination of this Residential Rental Agreement provided that: (A) no damages exist above normal wear and tear; (B) the Premises, including all carpets, walls, floors, appliances, and bathroom fixtures, have been thoroughly cleaned; (C) Resident allows Management to show Premises during the last sixty (60) days of this Residential Rental Agreement, provided that Management gives Resident at least 24 hours prior notice; (D) all monies due Management by Resident have been paid to Management; and (E) Resident has paid all final bills, including all utility bills, that have been Resident's responsibility during this Residential Rental Agreement.

8. SUBLETTING. Resident agrees that it will not assign, sublet, or transfer the Property or any part thereof without the Management's prior written consent.

9. UTILITIES. Resident shall be responsible and pay for all utilities and other services supplied to the Property.

10. CONDITION OF PROPERTY. Resident agrees that the Property is in a condition satisfactory for the purposes herein contemplated and that the same is accepted without warranty or representation as to condition on the part of Management.

11. INSURANCE. Management and/or the owner of the Property (the "Owner") has an insurance policy on the structure of the Property only. Resident is responsible for insurance on the contents of the Property and is encouraged to obtain renter's insurance to cover such contents prior to taking occupancy of the Property. In the case of damage to the Property, Resident is to notify Management immediately. If the Property is totally destroyed or so

substantially damaged as to be untenantable by storm, fire, earthquake, flooding, or other casualty, this Residential Rental Agreement shall terminate as of the date of such destruction or damage, and rental shall be accounted for as of that date between Management and Resident. If the Property should be damaged, but not be rendered untenantable: (A) to the extent that Management decides to make the requisite repairs, then Resident shall continue to pay Rent as normal under this Residential Rental Agreement; or (B) to the extent that Management decides not to make the requisite repairs, then the term of this Residential Rental Agreement shall end and the Rent shall be prorated up to the time of the damage.

12. MAINTENANCE. The maintenance of the property shall be done by the Resident to keep the property in good condition. The Resident shall be careful to ensure that the plumbing pipes do not freeze or are not clogged. Resident is prohibited from adding locks to, changing, or in any way altering locks installed on the doors on the Premises without the prior written consent of Management, and Resident shall provide Management copies of keys to the added, changed, or altered locks if Management does provide such consent. Resident acknowledges the presence of a working smoke detector on each level of the Premises and acknowledges that it understands how to test and operate the detector(s), and Resident agrees to test the detector(s) weekly for proper operation and replace batteries when necessary. Resident further agrees to notify Management immediately in writing if any detector fails to operate properly during any test. The refrigerator and window air conditioner, if any, delivered with the Premises are for the convenience of the Resident, but are not guaranteed to operate properly for the duration of the Residential Rental Agreement, and Resident agrees to be responsible for any repairs related to the operation of any such appliance. In the event Resident fails to maintain the lawns or shrubbery of the Property properly, Management, after attempting to notify Resident, may, but is not required to, maintain such lawns and/or shrubbery as Management deems proper, with all costs of such maintenance by Management to be paid by Resident.

13. EVICTION. If the Rent called for in Section 4 herein has not been paid by the Rent Due Date or Resident has failed to perform any term of this Residential Rental Agreement hereof, then Management shall, within two (2) days after providing notice to Resident thereof which has not been cured, automatically and immediately have the right to take out a Dispossessory Warrant and have Resident, his family, and possessions, evicted from the Premises. Whenever under the terms hereof Management is entitled to possession of Premises, Resident will at once surrender same to Management in good condition as at present, ordinary wear and tear excepted, and Resident will remove all of Resident's effects therefrom; and Management may forthwith reenter Premises and remove all persons and effects therefrom using such force as may be necessary without being guilty of forcible entry or detainer, trespass, or other tort.

(continued)

14. ABANDONMENT. If Resident removes or attempts to remove property from the Premises other than in the usual course of continuing occupancy, without having first paid Management all monies due, the Premises may be considered abandoned, and Management shall have the right, without notice, to store or dispose of any property left on the Premises by Resident. Management shall also have the right to store or dispose of any of the Resident's property remaining on the Premises after the termination of this Residential Rental Agreement. The title of any such property shall automatically vest in the Owner. Management may, at his option, declare this Residential Rental Agreement forfeited and rerent the Premises without any liability to Resident whatsoever.

15. ALTERATIONS. Resident shall not make, or allow to be made, any alterations, installations, or redecorations of any kind to the Property without prior written consent of Management; provided, however, that notwithstanding such consent, all alterations including items affixed to the Property shall become a permanent part of the Property and the property of the Owner upon the termination of the Residential Rental Agreement.

16. RIGHT OF ACCESS. Management has the right to access the Property during reasonable hours without notice to Resident for maintenance of the Property and for inspection to determine that the Property is being used for the purpose herein described and to determine the condition of the Property. In case of emergency, Management may enter the Property at any time.

17. ATTORNEY'S FEES. In any legal action to enforce any term under this Residential Rental Agreement, the prevailing party shall be entitled to all costs incurred in connection with such action, including reasonable attorney's fees and court costs.

18. LIMITATION ON LIABILITY AND INDEMNIFICATION. Management and Owner shall not be liable for any damage or injury to Resident, or any other person, or to any property occurring on the Property or in common areas thereof, unless such damage is the proximate result of the negligence or unlawful act of Management and Owner. Resident hereby indemnifies, releases, and holds harmless Management, Owner, and their agents from and against any and all suits, actions, claims, judgments, and expenses arising out of or relating to any damage or injury occurring on the Property or in connection with this Residential Rental Agreement, except for those acts described above.

19. WAIVER AND SEVERABILITY. No failure of Management to enforce any term of this Residential Rental Agreement shall be deemed a waiver, nor shall any acceptance of a partial payment of rent (or any payment marked "payment in full" or a similar designation) be deemed a waiver of Management's right to the full amount thereof. In the event that any part of this Residential Rental Agreement is deemed to be unenforceable by a court of law, the remaining parts of this Residential Rental Agreement shall remain in full force and effect

as though the unenforceable part or parts were not written into this Residential Rental Agreement.

In witness whereof, the parties hereto have caused this Residential Rental Agreement to be signed in person or by a person duly authorized, on the day and year above. No modifications may be made to this Residential Rental Agreement unless all parties agree in writing.

"MANAGEMENT"   **"RESIDENT"**

_____   _____

_____   _____

_____

_____

SAMPLE OPTION TO PURCHASE AGREEMENT

Note: For more details on this, refer to Chapter 13, "The Lease/Purchase Contract."

OPTION TO PURCHASE AGREEMENT

This agreement (hereinafter referred to as the "Option to Purchase Agreement") is made by _____ (hereinafter referred to as "Owner") in consideration of, among others, the faithful compliance by _____ (hereinafter referred to as "Resident") in connection with the terms of the attached Residential Rental Agreement and, specifically, the proper maintenance of the residential property located at _____ (hereinafter referred to as the "Property"). The full legal description of the Property is the same as is recorded with the _____ County, _____ and is made a part of this Option to Purchase Agreement by reference.

1. EXPIRATION. Resident has the option to purchase the Property on or before _____. This Option to Purchase Agreement shall automatically expire and be considered void after this date.

2. FINANCIAL TERMS. The financial terms of this Option to Purchase Agreement shall be:

   a. *Purchase Price.* If Resident exercises its option to purchase the Property, Owner agrees to sell the Property to Resident for the purchase price of _____ Dollars ($_____).

   b. *Money for Consideration.* Resident shall pay Owner _____ Dollars ($_____) as money for consideration for the option to purchase the Property under this Option to Purchase Agreement. This Money for Consideration may be applied towards the Purchase of the Property. However, in the instance that resident chooses not to exercise this Option to Purchase Agreement, then the Money for Consideration shall automatically and immediately vest with Owner in total.

   c. *Applied Rent.* From each month's Rent under the Residential Rental Agreement, Owner agrees to apply _____ Dollars ($___) toward Resident's purchase of the Property. However, the Applied Rent shall be nonrefundable to Resident and shall automatically and immediately vest with Owner, in total, in the instance that Resident chooses not to exercise this Option to Purchase Agreement.

   d. *Payment Schedule.*

3. NOTICE. Resident must notify Owner in writing of its intent to exercise this Option to Purchase Agreement no later than fifteen (15) days before exercising the option to purchase under this Option to Purchase Agreement.

4. ASSIGNMENT. This Option to Purchase Agreement is not transferable or assignable to any third party by Resident, and can only be exercised by the Resident signing this Option to Purchase Agreement.

5. CONVEYANCE. Upon Resident exercising its option to purchase under this Option to Purchase Agreement, the Property shall be conveyed by Owner to Resident via a warranty deed subject to all easements and other restrictions of record.

6. CONDITION OF PROPERTY. Resident agrees that the Property is in condition satisfactory for the purposes herein contemplated and that the same is accepted without warranty or representation as to condition on the part of Owner.

7. REPAIRS, IMPROVEMENTS, AND ASSOCIATION FEES. During the term of this Option to Purchase Agreement and the Residential Rental Agreement, as further consideration, Resident agrees to be responsible and pay for all repairs and improvements and to refrain from any acts or lack of actions which might result in any jeopardy or loss of value to the Property. This includes painting, maintenance of mechanical, electrical, plumbing, heating, and cooling systems, lawn, shrubbery, interior and exterior walls, doors, roof, and anything else necessary to prevent the Property from deteriorating in any manner and to keep the Property in good condition. However, Resident agrees not to make any major repairs and improvements without obtaining the prior written consent of Owner. Resident also agrees to be responsible and pay for all homeowners association fees, including swimming and tennis fees. Resident is also responsible for all pest control.

8. EVICTION. If the Rent called for in Section 4 of the Residential Rental Agreement is past due, then Owner shall have the right to evict Resident as set forth in Section 13 of the Residential Rental Agreement and terminate this Option to Purchase Agreement.

9. ATTORNEY'S FEES AND CLOSING COSTS. In any legal action to enforce any term under this Residential Rental Agreement, the prevailing party shall be entitled to all costs incurred in connection with such action, including reasonable attorney's fees and court costs. Upon Resident exercising its option to purchase under this Option to Purchase Agreement, Resident agrees to pay all closing costs, including attorney's fees, transfer fees, and recordation fees, in connection with the purchase of the Property.

10. WAIVER. No failure of Owner to enforce any term of this Option to Purchase Agreement shall be deemed a waiver.

In witness whereof, the parties hereto have caused this Option to Purchase Agreement to be signed in person or by a person duly authorized, on the day and year below. No

(continued)

modifications may be made to this Option to Purchase Agreement unless all parties agree in writing.

ACCEPTED AS WRITTEN THIS DATE _____

"MANAGEMENT"   **"RESIDENT"**

_____   _____

_____   _____

_____

_____

SAMPLE SAVED MONEY LETTER

Note: For more details on this, refer to Chapter 14, "Managing Lease/Purchase Relationships."

_____

_____

_____

_____

_____

_____

Dear _____:

As of _____, for the property located at the above-referenced address, you have:

Accumulated Applied Rent	$_____
Option Money	$_____
Security Deposit	$_____
Total	$_____

If you have any questions, please feel free to give us a call at _____.

Sincerely,

_____

SAMPLE NOTICE OF LATE RENT LETTER

Note: For more details on this, refer to Chapter 14, "Managing Lease/Purchase Relationships."

VIA CERTIFIED MAIL

NOTICE OF LATE RENT

Property: _____

Residents: _____

Date: _____

    A review of our records indicates that we have not received your rent for the month of _____ for the above-referenced property.

    If we do not receive the sum of $_____

    representing the unpaid rental in the amount of $_____

    plus late fees in the amount of $_____

    Within 24 hours of your receipt of this notice, a dispossessory warrant will be taken out and other necessary legal action will be taken to collect all money due on this claim (including the cost of the warrant and all court costs and attorney's fees), recover possession of the property, and exercise all other remedies provided by your lease agreement and by law.

    The above amount must be paid in the form of cashier's check or money order and a copy faxed to _____ _____-_____ and the original then immediately mailed. The amount stated above must be paid at management's address, which is shown below.

    Notified by: _____

    Management: _____

    Address: _____

SAMPLE LEASE/PURCHASE EXTENSION AMENDMENT

Note: For more details on this, refer to Chapter 14, "Managing Lease/Purchase Relationships."

LEASE/PURCHASE EXTENSION AMENDMENT

This agreement (hereinafter referred to as the "Amendment") is made between _____ (hereinafter referred to as "Management/Owner") and _____ (hereinafter referred to as "Resident") in connection with the Residential Rental Agreement and Option to Purchase Agreement dated _____ (the "Lease/Purchase Agreement") for the property located at _____ (hereinafter referred to as the "Property").

1. TERM AND EXPIRATION. Section 1 of the Residential Rental Agreement and Section 1 of the Option to Purchase Agreement are hereby amended to automatically enter a period of one-year renewals ("Renewal Periods") effective _____, wherein Renewal Periods shall automatically continue for additional periods of one year unless either Management/Owner or Resident notifies the other in writing of its intent to terminate the Lease/Purchase Agreement at least ninety (90) days prior to the end of the then current Renewal Period.

2. MONIES PREVIOUSLY ACCUMULATED. Section 2B of the Option to Purchase Agreement is hereby amended so that all monies previously accumulated by Resident under the Option to Purchase Agreement shall still be available to Resident only if Resident chooses to exercise the Option to Purchase Agreement to purchase the Property. Otherwise all such monies previously accumulated shall be nonrefundable to Resident and shall immediately and automatically vest with Owner. After payment of _____ rent (assuming all rent payments are current), $_____ shall be available to Resident toward Resident's purchase of the Property should Resident choose to exercise the Option to Purchase Agreement. The $_____ represents $_____ of Applied Rent plus $_____ of Option Money plus $_____ of Security Deposit.

3. FIRST RENEWAL PERIOD. Sections 4 and 5 of the Residential Rental Agreement and Sections 2A and 2B of the Option to Purchase Agreement are hereby amended so that in the first Renewal Period, the Rent and Purchase Price will remain unchanged. However, Management/Owner shall not apply any portion of the payments in connection with the Rent towards the purchase of the Property during this first Renewal Period.

4. SECOND AND FUTURE RENEWAL PERIODS. Sections 4 and 5 of the Residential Rental Agreement and sections 2A and 2B of the Option to Purchase Agreement are hereby amended so that, beginning with the second Renewal Period and for all Renewal Periods thereafter, the Rent and Purchase Price will increase by ____ percent (___%) per period

(continued)

over each prior period's Rent and Purchase Price amounts. However, Management will continue not to apply any portion of the payments in connection with the Rent toward the purchase of the Property during these Renewal Periods.

5. REMAINDER OF TERMS UNCHANGED. Management/Owner and Resident further acknowledge and agree that all other terms of the Lease/Purchase Agreement remain unchanged.

"MANAGEMENT/OWNER"   **"RESIDENT"**   **"RESIDENT"**

_____   _____   _____

_____   _____   _____

Date   **Date**   **Date**

SAMPLE OPTION TO PURCHASE SALES SUMMARY

Note: For more details on this, refer to Chapter 15, "Selling Your Homes."

Option to Purchase Sales Summary for:

_____

_____

_____

_____

Dear Closing Attorney,

The following are the specifics for the sale of the above-referenced property.

- *Sales Price.* $___

- *Option Money.* $___, to be applied towards down payment

- *Applied Rent.* $__/month × _ months of tenancy = $___ (to be applied toward down payment)

- *Security Deposit.* $___ (to be applied towards down payment)

- Buyer to pay all closing costs

The loan on the property is held by _____, phone number _____, loan #_____, and the seller's Social Security number is _____.
If you have questions, please do not hesitate to call the seller at _____.

Sincerely,

_____